T0337913

What Distinguishes Human Understanding?

What Distinguishes Human Understanding?

John Deely

ST. AUGUSTINE'S PRESS
South Bend, Indiana
2002

1 2 3 4 5 6   07 06 05 04 03 02

Library of Congress Cataloging in Publication Data
Deely, John N.
    What distinguishes human understanding? / John
    Deely.
      p. cm.
    Includes bibliographical references and index.
    ISBN 1-890318-97-3 (alk. paper)
    1. Philosophy of mind. 2. Comprehension.
    3. Semiotics. I. Title.
BD418.3 D44 2000
128'.2 – dc21   00-008721

∞ *The paper used in this publication meets the minimum requirements of the International
Organisation for Standardization (ISO) - Paper for documents - Requirements for permanence
- ISO 9706: 1994.*

Printed in the Czech Republic by Newton Printing Ltd. www.newtonprinting.com

This book is dedicated

to Timm, with two "m"s,

the first for his spouse Mary,

the second for his children Mitchell & Madeline

Contents

Foreword

This is an essay in what used to be, and still largely is, called the "philosophy of mind", a designation heavy with the dualistic assumptions of classical modernity. When those assumptions wrapped up in that traditional classification are jettisoned in favor of an epistemological paradigm compossible with semiosis, it becomes clear that what we are dealing with is straightforwardly a semiotics of the cognitive activities of living organisms. The following pages are better viewed under this clarification.

Dr. Anthony Russell claimed that the clarification makes of the essay "the first treatment of the distinction between sense and intellect worth reading since the days of Locke and Hume". Be that as it may, if the reader adjudges the work worth having read, the game shall have been worth the candle.

Semiotics is nothing more or other than the knowledge we develop by studying the action of signs, and it receives its various divisions from the various ways and regions in which that action is verified. This study presupposes nothing more than a notion of sign as one thing standing for another in a relation of *renvoi*, that is to say, an irreducibly triadic relation, actual or virtual, but in the case of cognitive life, it seems, always actual. Such a general notion of sign is verified, at the extremes, in phenomena we call "natural" and in phenomena we call "cultural", as well as in the intermediary phenomena of social interaction such as sociology, for example, studies it. But – and this is one of the more surprising upshots of contemporary semiotic research – the actual proposal of such a general notion of sign appears to be no older than Augustine, and a creation of the specifically Latin Age of philosophical history.

Proposed at the end of the fourth century, the semiotic point of view did not receive a warrant until the early seventeenth century, when it was for the first time demonstrated how the early Latin proposal for a general notion of sign, applicable in a single sense to the extremes of nature and culture, could be vindicated through the fact that relation according to the way it has being is indifferent to whether its subjective foundation or ground be taken from physical interaction and being or from cognitive activity alone. This establishment of a unified object or subject matter for semiotic investigation was in principle revolutionary for our understanding of human experience and the knowledge which derives therefrom. It unified in a single instrument or medium the otherwise diverse products of speculative knowledge about the natures of things and practical knowledge about human affairs and the application thereto of speculative knowledge.

The first author who succeeded in giving voice to the underlying unity of the being in relation upon which all action of signs as such depends was John Poinsot (1589–1644), an Iberian philosopher of mixed Burgundian and Portuguese descent. In the text of his *Tractatus de Signis*, published in 1632, the new beginning implicit in the adoption of the semiotic point of view is in two ways at least symbolized. First, the text expressly notes that the sign requires a standpoint superior to the division of being into what is and what is not independent of cognition, which translates, in modern parlance, into a standpoint superior to the confrontation of realism with idealism. Second, the compass of the *Tractatus de Signis* text unites what were, in the then-traditional liberal arts curriculum of the European universities, the opening discussions of logic with the concluding discussions of the theory of knowledge.

>x<

This new beginning, the way of signs, was not, however, the new beginning that the authors of what was to become the classical modern mainstream of philosophy actually undertook. Instead, they chose to follow what Leibniz summarily and accurately characterized, in 1704, as the way of ideas. This historical path was predicated on the assumption that the very ideas formed by the human mind are as such the immediate and direct objects of experience at every level of cognitive activity – that is to say, in sensation no less than in intellection as the activity proper to human understanding. This assumption, however, which is the heart of the modern epistemological paradigm, is impossible in semiotic terms, because it depends upon a reduction of signification to representation. Such a reduction had already been shown to be a confusion by a whole series of late Latin authors, principally Hispanic, who had undertaken in the fifteenth and sixteenth centuries the initial exploration and development of the requirements of semiotic consciousness. But their work was unknown to the founders of philosophical modernity. In the glare of attention focused on the way of ideas, the way of signs, barely adumbrated by authors of a waning Latinity, soon became lost in the shadows of modernity's waxing, and remained forgotten until a confluence of scholarly coincidences, themselves mostly occasioned by the contemporary interest in semiotic studies, brought them to light.

In the ancient world dominated by Greek philosophy, the notion we translate as sign, σημεῖον ("semeion"), should actually be translated rather as *"natural sign"*, for this term in antiquity referred only to natural phenomena such as meteorological occurrences and symptoms of disease. When attention was finally turned to the phenomena of signification in late modern times – in the very twilight of modernity in which mainstream philosophy of the twentieth century persists in dwelling – there was hardly any place left for a viable notion of natural phenomenon. It was therefore no accident that the original popular success of contemporary attempts to develop a theory of sign was not under the designation of *semiotics*, a name redolent of the natural origins of signification in physical processes anterior to human cognition. The attempts which caught the public eye went rather under the designation of *semiology*, a name taken from linguistic studies and intended to signify that the paradigm for any theory of signs should be not the early Latin general notion but a specifically modern notion of sign as determinately arbitrary and linguistic, that is, cultural, in derivation.

Only slowly and against the greatest resistance on all sides did semiotic research, indebted especially to the powerful impulse given it by the philosophical investigations in this area by Charles Sanders Peirce, compel the gradual recognition on all sides that any notion of sign as inherently arbitrary, however valid and necessary in specific areas, was incapable of providing an adequate foundation for the possible field of investigations opened up by the action of signs. The progress of this grudging recognition was signalled in the literature on signs, iconically, as it were, by the shift in terminology from "semiology" to "semiotics" as the proper designation for the point of view under development. The two continue to be confused in the popular culture, as is inevitable for a time, by authors who superficially see in the two terms merely alternate designations for the same general idea.[1]

Thus, by the most unexpected of turns in philosophical history, semiotics as the way of signs puts us back at a point where modern philosophy began, and compels us to look anew at the late Latin-early modern texts, ignored by modernity, wherein was achieved the first establishment of the foundations for what we today call semiotics. From this curious standpoint, at once antiquarian and postmodern, as I have elsewhere explained,[2] is the present essay written. It is an essay, as I say, in the semiotics of the cognitive activity of organisms. This is how a semiotician expresses, in terms of the

---

[1] Thus Michael Dirda, in a book review for the *Washington Post Book World* for October 22, 1995, ignorantly defines semiotics as "the study of cultural 'signs'" – a definition strictly applicable only to semiology as subalternate to, as a part only of, the much vaster study of sign action in the universe at large properly called semiotics.

[2] Deely 1984 and esp. 1994a.

triadic structure of signs, the traditional discipline called "philosophy of mind" – a name connoting the never successfully defended modern postulation of a mind-body dualism which semiotics begins by rejecting or, perhaps better to say, by quite ignoring.

If I ignore, practically speaking, the main body of literature developed in recent years under, or at least presupposing the background of, the dualistic assumptions of modernity, I do so because whatever that literature has to contribute to semiotic consciousness will be possible to sort out only gradually, after the semiotic point of view has been clearly established on its own ground and terms. Since this book is theoretical, I have taken my orientation not from any literature alien in origin to the semiotic point of view. I have used as my principal guide systematic reflection upon the function of signs in our experience taken in their own right (semiosis) as superior to the divisions of being into natural and cultural phenomena.

To the extent that I have relied on any authority, it has not been, therefore, the authority of any author considered as belonging to the paradigm of some particular tradition prejacent to semiotics, but of the author – or rather, the text of the author[3] – who first succeeded in envisioning and formulating explicitly the requirements which most properly define the perspective of semiotics in terms of the underlying unity of its principal object of investigation or subject matter. Nor have I hesitated to go beyond that author's text where the pragmaticistic clarification of how semiosis achieves its structuring and development of human experience and knowledge (even in its most benighted and mistaken byways) requires the breaking of new ground.

Recognizing that the original Latin text in which the unity of semiotic inquiry was originally demonstrated is not easy to read in the best of circumstances, I have taken the trouble to append in footnotes, added after my essay was written, the principal texts from that work which bear on my theme. These texts have nowhere else been so gathered, and I have found

---

[3] Which is not quite the same thing, after all.

the exercise of thus bringing them into focus highly instructive – as will, I hope, the reader. Rather than presuppose in the reader an ability to handle the Latin directly, I have preceded these textual citations in every case with an English translation. The text of Poinsot's *Tractatus de Signis* of 1632 used throughout this work is that of the 1985 bilingual edition I published through the University of California Press, the first such independent edition in the history of the work, as there explained (Deely 1985). Page and line numbers, separated by a dash, as cited in the present book refer directly to the left-hand or English column of text, although I very occasionally tinker with the translation. Since the Latin and English columns of this edition of the *Tractatus* begin and end within the same line of text on every page, the line numbers to the English are accurate also for the Latin within three lines or usually less. Even the scholarly reader interested primarily in the Latin original will hardly be inconvenienced by the preference here given to the line numbers as they key directly the English column of text.

There will be time enough for a scholarly assessment, or, rather, reassessment, of late modern literature under the light of semiotics, in the so-called "philosophy of mind" as everywhere else. The present requires something quite different: a clear establishment of the perspective of semiotics on its own grounds. And this, in fulfillment of the promissory note on p. 117 of *Introducing Semiotic*, I have here tried to accomplish for the area of human understanding in what distinguishes it.

John Deely
completed with a "Friend of Len Provisor" Parker pen,
corrections with a Pilot "vanishing point",
in the Colonia Santa Maria Ahuacatitlán,
Casa de Alberto Diaz de Cossio, el Ceramista.
Cuernavaca, Morelos, México,
on the "feast of the Holy Innocents"
28 December 1995;
final revision in Houston, Texas, Graustark House
in connection with the University of St. Thomas,
28 January 2000

What Distinguishes
Human Understanding?

Preamble

One of the oldest philosophical discussions of which we have record concerns the relation of human intelligence to the intelligence exhibited by other biological forms, especially, of course, animal forms high on the scale of life as judged by similarity to ourselves, what Ralph Austin Powell used to term "the humanesque analogy". The bottom line in this discussion always comes down to the question of whether there is a qualitative difference in kind separating human understanding from the "understanding" or intelligence of other animal species, or merely a quantitative difference of complexity and degree? The situation is like pregnancy: either the woman is pregnant or she is not, regardless of how far along the pregnancy may be. So, similarly, either anthropos has an understanding species-specifically distinct in kind which further admits of degrees,[1] or human intelligence is simply – nothing more than – the manifestation in varying degrees of modalities of apprehension that are also to be found elsewhere in the animal world.

Discussion of the issue has normally been muddied by the fact that few of the participants actually cared a whit about the

---

[1] Just as a woman can be pregnant in varying degrees only if she is pregnant, but cannot be pregnant in varying degrees if she is not pregnant.

communication systems of the animals other than human. Their concern was most often to assert "the uniqueness of man", often with a view to further conclusions about personal immortality, at least since the medieval rise of Christianity as a major influence on philosophical speculation; or, on the opposing side, to deny that uniqueness and all its implications, real or imagined.

Older than Aristotle, nonetheless, the question before us has always found proponents on either side of the binary issue. The issue was rendered more acute after the work of Darwin, which made the adoption of an evolutionary model for nature and mind all but unavoidable. Darwin conceived of all evolution as a matter of degrees of difference, and so, down to the present, have many others.

With the emergence of semiotics, I think it becomes possible to put this discussion on a whole new footing, to formulate the matter in terms of unprecedented clarity, and to resolve the issue without any reference to religious concerns or belief in some supposed "afterlife".

Chapter 1

Requirements of the Discussion

First of all, it is no longer possible to participate intelligently in this discussion without taking account of the fact that there are qualitative differences in the communication systems of all biological species or forms. Not only the human species, but, it would seem, every species exhibits species-specific modalities of apprehension and consequent communication.[1] So the question of whether human understanding differs qualitatively or only quantitatively from the cognition of other animals becomes to a large extent moot. Every cognitive organism belongs to one or another species, and every cognitive species is distinguished by apprehensive modalities peculiar to itself. This point is quite independent of the question of whether, underlying such differences, is not simply a difference in arrangement of basic material particles.

Of continuing relevance here is the Aristotelian idea of substance as the formal unity to which different material arrangements (of genes, in current parlance) give rise and which in turn makes that arrangement cohere as a unity so

---

[1]　For details, see Sebeok Ed. 1977; Sebeok 1978; Umiker-Sebeok and Sebeok 1979–1982; Sebeok and Umiker-Sebeok series 1979-; Umiker-Sebeok and Sebeok Eds. 1980; Sebeok and Rosenthal Eds. 1981.

>5<

long as the individual exists with a distinguishable identity. By way of anticipating one of the principal rectifications of terms that the fuller development of semiotic consciousness requires, some remarks are in order already here regarding this term "substance".

So far as this term was original with Aristotle and came into later general use among the Latin scholastics, despite a misleading characterization of the abstract situation of individuality in terms of an "absolute" subject or being, "substance" conveyed the notion of an individual (even as merely possible) capable of actual existence only through a network of environmental relations (by definition "physical") within which (or at whose center) would be sustained the intrinsic unity of the individual (its "substantial form") as relatively independent respecting this or that of its circumstances. Later modifications of Aristotle's original conception of substance transformed it from a notion having positional as well as self-referential or "absolute" value into the notion of something wholly self-contained, as we find in the work of Kant and, typically, throughout the rationalist works of the classical moderns. This rationalist transformation led directly to the rejection of the notion of substance among the empiricists.

Since this is one of the fulcrum points on which the development of semiotics turns away from classical modernity (or, as might also be said, on which the classical development of modernity turned away from the nascent semiotics of the closing Latin centuries), it is worth being as clear as possible on what is at stake in these two very different significations, the ancient and the modern ones – verging on, if not actually achieving, equivocation – conveyed by the misleadingly "same" word (or, rather, character string) "substance". Clarification of the contrast is all the more called for in view of the fact that the actual focus of modern philosophy on epistemological concerns pushes into the background and, effectively, hides the basic question of prejacent connections among physical things in the environment by the fact that, as Handyside well observed,[2] "the things are no longer the independently conceived

---

[2] Handyside 1929: x.

substances of intellect, but the conjointly perceived objects of sense". But if we look at those of Kant's writings that preceded and laid the ground for the celebrated *Critiques* which established his place as Master of Modernity, we find, as clearly as in Descartes or in Leibniz, that pragmaticisticly insupportable notion of substance, the "monad without windows", which came to occupy the field of modern philosophy. Kant puts the matter thus:[3]

> Since every self-sufficient being contains within itself the complete source of all its determinations, it is not necessary for its existence that it stand in relation to other things. Substances can therefore exist, and yet have no outer relation to things, nor stand in any actual connection with them.

A notion so remote from experience hardly justifies supplanting entirely the original notion of substance as derived from the experience of changing individuals, in view of which experience the notion was fashioned by Aristotle to provide the ground for understanding the difference between those changes which any given individual does and those which it does not survive. Cut loose from all reference to experience, Kant is able to *deduce* from *his* notion of the individual substance conclusions which Aristotle only *abduced* of the physical universe or "world" as a whole, such as that it has no "place" where it exists (no *ubi circumsriptivum*), and "other propositions, which are not less remarkable, and which capture the understanding so to speak against its own will".[4] (It would be hard to find a better capsule summary of modern philosophy.)

This perverse development, nonetheless, should not be allowed to gainsay the value of the original notion of substance not as something entirely self-contained but merely as something self-identified within a network of external contingencies

---

[3] Kant 1747: 8.
[4] Kant *loc. cit.*

from which the individual has both existence and place. This individuality, being relative from the outset and throughout, therefore, can be more or less pronounced. It is empirically the more pronounced as we ascend in observation the scale of being from those material particles and interactions for which we have no empirical grounds for abducing the presence of life to those forms where life becomes more and more clearly evident as a warranted abduction, ending in ourselves where our very existence as thinking beings is its own warrant – this I think is the enduring value of the Cartesian formula, *Cogito ergo sum*. For while it is equally true of any action – drinking, running, breathing – that the action implies existence (*agere sequitur esse* was the way the medievals epitomized the general situation), yet the action of thinking as involving a self-awareness, a reflective activity which has itself for its own object, is the premier action where an existing and living subject grasps itself, makes a part of its own physical reality an object. In this case physical existence not only intrudes itself as such as part of the objective realm (the order of whatever exists as known), but to be a thing partly objectified is also to be oneself.

Here, as we shall see more fully in what follows, in the awareness of the self by the self we find vindicated those arcane early semiotic discussions of the difference between, on the one hand, the experience of objects which have as such a physical dimension within their very objectification here and now and, on the other hand, objects cognized without an accompanying verification here and now of any such dimensions. This pragmaticistic difference was clumsily labeled "intuitive versus abstractive cognition" under the historical determinism of the transitional influence of Duns Scotus[5] who, toward the opening of the 14th century, turns Latin epistemological and ontological discussions in the semiotic direction that would culminate in the early 17th century *Tractatus de Signis* of Poinsot[6] at the very moment that Descartes turned

[5] See Tachau 1988: 70, 80 ff.
[6] See the *Tractatus de Signis*, Book III, Questions 1 and 2; and see also Beuchot and Deely 1995.

what was to become the classical modern development toward the dead-end of an idealism confining the mind to its own workings (classical modern idealism, common to Rationalism and Empiricism in their fatal shared assumption reducing signification to representation in the idea of ideas of human understanding). We shall see in discussing below the semiosis of sensation that, *pace* Descartes, the experience of the self by the self in reflective thought is far from the only instance where the subjective or physical as such is transformed, by the simple addition of a cognitive relation to a cognitive organism, into something objective. In sensation generally, just as in the reflective grasp of the self thinking, something existing subjectively becomes the focus of an "intuitive apprehension"; only now, in place of (though along with, as we shall see) the self some aspects of the physical environment here and now impinging on a cognitive organism are apprehended as so impinging. Indeed, it is just this paradigm case of sensory experience that the possibility of reflection on the self presupposes. But let us not get ahead of the story.

In modern philosophy, the notion of intuition has come to be more or less completely discredited. No one has made this point more abundantly than the principal progenitor of contemporary semiotics, Charles Sanders Peirce, in his 1868–1869 series of articles on intuitive knowledge (so Burks 1958: 261 describes the series) in the then-recently founded *Journal of Speculative Philosophy*. But, where intuitive awareness in the Latin sense was expounded in the original systematization of semiotic foundations essayed under the title of *Tractatus de Signis*,[7] as the Peirce scholar, Michael Raposa, has recently demonstrated in detail, "appearances are deceptive and there is no fundamental disagreement between the two philosophers" – Charles Peirce and John Poinsot – either "on this

---

[7] Book III *Concerning Modes of Awareness and Concepts*, Question 1 "Whether Intuitive and Abstractive Awareness Differ Essentially in the Rationale of Cognition" and Question 2 "Whether There Can Be an Intuitive Cognition, either in the Understanding or in Exterior Sense, of a Thing Physically Absent".

issue" or on the issue of introspection.[8] To follow the details of Raposa, Poinsot, and Peirce simply on this matter of terminology would lead us by many steps outside our present path of reflection. Suffice it to mark here, as a reference for other researchers,[9] that in the terminology of "intuition" and "intuitive awareness" we encounter another of those fulcral points at which classical modern philosophy sharply turned away from any semiotic development of consciousness in favor of a view of mental representation which could have no other outcome than candid solipsism or decadent skepticism. The change of significations behind the mask of a continuity in literal form is, in this area, every bit as dramatic as the change we noted in more detail – because more directly in the line of our present concern – on the character string "substance".

Yet another fulcral point of terminology. We need to note here specifically that there was among the Latins a fragmentary and only implicitly systematic use of the term "objective", which was consistent with their original use of the notion of sign as applicable to natural and cultural phenomena alike. In modern philosophy this use came to be quite reversed. This reversed use, wherein "objective" becomes synonymous with what is the case apart from any opinion, thoroughly established by our own time, nonetheless proves incompatible with the general doctrine of signs and is, I would go so far as to say, ultimately incoherent. This incoherence is what we see at play at the level of popular culture in the inane debates about whether reporting can or should be "objective", as also, more fundamentally, in the interminable struggle within modern philosophy between "realisms" and "idealisms", a struggle which continues to confuse and delay semiotic developments. Semiotics in effect compels us to resume the nascent medieval notion of objective as whatever exists as known, but now to thematize and systematize that

---

[8] Raposa 1994: 396; see further esp. 399–402.

[9] The interested reader will find pieces of the story in Deely 1985: 485–87, Raposa 1994, and Deely 1994a; but the story as a whole remains – perhaps for some ambitious doctoral student – to tell as a whole.

usage in light of the discovery that the sign is what every object presupposes. This backward step, as it were, is for the sake of two steps forward.[10] In any event, the *Cogito* is simply the fixed point, among a synechistic continuity of contingent points at every moment of experience, where a coincidence of the two orders of objective and physical being is always inescapable – a situation quite different from that which Descartes tortured the data to construe,[11] and one to which is pertinent the idea, called "intuitive" by the Latins, of cognition as the awareness of a physical aspect of the environment as such here and now part of the sensory core of perception and understanding.

This terminological point may be regarded as preliminary to what is the point crucial to our present consideration, to wit, that awareness, whether reflective or not, whether turned toward or away from the immediate physical surroundings, belongs to the formal dimension or side of organismic life. Whatever it may presuppose on the material side, and however much it may depend on that material organization in order to enter or continue in existence, it cannot be reduced to an identity with the material without the organism ceasing to be. True, there have been those, at least as far back as Thales (c.640–546BC), who professed to see no essential difference between living and dead. (He defended his preference for life over death on the grounds that "there is no difference"[12]). But we cannot take responsibility for the thought of others. Confronted with the corpse of a friend, few would deny that something was missing, and that this something took along

[10] Retrieving the signification of objectivity consistent with the perspective of semiotics was part of the essential project of *The Human Use of Signs* (Deely 1994), and I continue it here.

[11] That the experience of the *cogito* points rather to embodiment than, as Descartes tried to argue, to disembodiment was most effectively demonstrated, perhaps, in the phenomenological work of Merleau-Ponty; but one of the best attacks upon the problem from within semiotics has been that of Greimas and Fontanille 1991. See the "Foreword" to the English trans. of this work by Perron and Fabbri 1993.

[12] As reported (c.220 AD) by Diogenes Laertius, "Thales" viii.

with itself awareness on the side of the material remains. On the side of the corpse, there is no more *cogito.*

Our thinking, of course, *pace* Descartes, is hardly what ensures our existence. Our existence is ensured by the environmental conditions including relations without which its possibility – the possibility of ourselves as thinking beings – would be removed. These conditions are indeed material, beginning with the air we breathe and the gravity which holds us to the earth, along with the surrounding temperature which enables our system to circulate and the atmospheric pressure which keeps us from exploding from the pressures within. Psychological conditions too are necessary to our sustenance, beginning with memory – "the closest link in the body with the self"[13] – without which there is no "I" to think. We may become, as they say, vegetables through some disaster or misfortune; we may exist without thinking. That is not the point. That we exist while thinking is all that thinking can assure.

This is another of the points at which semiotic thought departs definitively from the epistemology of classical modernity. To say that all thought is in signs is to say that all thought is of significates, that all ideas give rise to relations at whose suprasubjective term are the signified objects – whether mere objects or objects which are also things – which the ideas are not.[14] For nothing prevents an object signified from having

---

[13]   Sebeok 1988: 191.

[14]   This was the essential insight of the late Latin Hispanic thinkers (beginning at least as early as Soto, who may have taken the idea from his Paris professors) who founded their semiotic epistemology by sharply distinguishing representation as such from signification. They pointed out that, in the sign, the representative element as such does not constitute the sign but merely provides the foundation or basis upon which the pure relation in its proper character as suprasubjective constitutes the sign as terminating at a significate. In all cases, a significate is irreducibly other than the representation which founds its objectivity. These considerations are summarized at the very outset of the *Tractatus de Signis*. See esp. the 2nd Preliminary Chapter, 25/11–27/6; and Book I, Question 1, 116/14–117/17, 121/19–123/25, etc.

and revealing itself precisely within the signification – that is to say, as part and parcel with the significate – an existence which does not reduce to the signification. This is what the formula *cogito ergo sum* actually gets at when read semiotically: the self given in thinking is given as other than the thinking, even though accessed only through the thinking.[15] The complement of Descartes' maxim would appear to be Aristotle's maxim about perception: that when its objects are not present in sensation it is a mystery whether they continue physically to exist.[16] I went to the September 26–28, 1995, Conference on "Perception and Self-Consciousness in the Arts and Sciences" organized in Porto, Portugal, by Norma Tasca, for example, expecting to see Thomas Sebeok and hence assuming that, in the interim, he would continue to live. As it turned out, the expectation was happily justified; but it need not have been so, and one time a similar assumption may not be (assuming Sebeok predeceases me, which also need not be).

I cannot think without existing, and I cannot exist without an environment. Whenever I think, both my physical existence and something of my physical environment enter into my awareness. What in fact of my environment is objectified depends on what I am thinking about and where I am as well as upon my biological constitution. Thus the entrance of the environment into my awareness is more variable than the

---

[15] The disappearance of the self in a stream and flow of detached associations, images, and ideas, as portrayed by Hume and others, we may say, is a direct consequence of the classical modern failure to distinguish between representation as such and signification, which we noted above (note) as one of the cornerstones of semiotic thinking.

[16] Aristotle, c.335–4BC: Nicomachean Ethics VI, 139b20–22 (p. 1799): "of things capable of being otherwise we do not know, when they have passed outside our observation, whether they exist or not." Similarly, c.348–330BC: Met. VII, 1036a1–8 (p. 1635): "when we come to the concrete thing . . . whether sensible or intelligible . . . of these there is no definition, but they are known by the aid of thought or perception; and when they go out of our actual consciousness it is not clear whether they exist or not". See further in Ch. 6, note 34, p. 107, below.

entrance of myself, though there is always necessarily something of both. I am a necessary object of my own thought, or, perhaps better to say, my self is an aspect of objectivity as I think about anything whatever. I am the only particular object within my environment that is, in this sense, in all cases necessary. When I open my eyes in a conscious state, if I am not blind I will necessarily see something of what the surrounding physical conditions of light and circumstance dictate. When the moon is full and I am outdoors I cannot open my eyes with my head turned in that direction without seeing the moon, even though the question of what I am seeing – a planetary body in space, a giant cheese, a source of direct or reflected light, a body embedded in a rotating sphere – is another matter. In both cases, what is objectified – something of myself along with whatever part of the environment – is something that exists subjectively and physically, now made also to be objectively. But this is a pragmaticistic proposition, the statement of a discovery, of a realization, not the assertion of a dogma. How the discovery comes about, it seems to me, is the key to the difference between perception and understanding – between, to use the canonical terminology, "sense" and "intellect". And to see how this is so it is necessary to approach the matter from a semiotic point of view.

A semiotic point of view is fundamentally one which takes its origin from the consideration of the action of signs as its first object, its primary focus. From within this point of view, of course, many methods or further standpoints are possible.[17] If we may credit the testimony of the first thinker to systematize initial requirements of such a point of view, the first requirement is to adopt a standpoint which transcends the difference between objects which have also a physical existence and objects which have only an objective existence; for the sign, as giving to experience whatever structure it has including the sheerly biologically determined, is our avenue equally to both sorts of object.[18] It is only through the use of

[17] See "Semiotics: Method or Point of View?" in Deely 1990: 9–21.

[18] *Tractatus de Signis*, Book I, Question 1, 117/28–118/18: "And we speak here of ontological relation – of relation according to the way it has

signs that we come to realize any distinction between the physical, the objectified physical, and the merely objective. To ground such distinctions it is necessary rightly to construe the nature proper to signs as relative beings.

For the remainder of my discussion here I am going to proceed on the assumption that the standpoint adopted for the *Tractatus de Signis* should be taken seriously. By this I do not mean to say that I am going to presuppose the validity of Poinsot's doctrine and proceed from there, but rather to say that I am going to begin with the *primum semeioticum* as expressed in the text of his *Tractatus de Signis* and proceed to explore its implications for the interpretation of experience. In this way, the "assumption" of validity, far from being "taken for granted in what follows", functions heuristically in such wise that, in the course of the very discussion it originates, it must become self-refuting or critically validated. As to which of the two, the final decision is left to you the reader.

being – not of a determinately physical relation as such, because we are discussing the sign in general, as it includes equally the natural and the social sign, in which general discussion even the signs which are mental artifacts – namely, conventional signs as such – are involved. And for this reason, the rationale common to signs cannot be that of a categorial being, i.e. a being restricted as such to the physical order, nor a determinately physical relation as such, although it could be an ontological relation, a relation according to the way it has being [inasmuch as relation so considered] is purely a relation and does not import anything absolute". – "Et loquimur hic de relatione secundum esse, non de relatione praedicamentali, quia loquimur de signo in communi, prout includit tam signum naturale quam ad placitum, in quo involvitur etiam signum, quod est aliquid rationis, scilicet signum ad placitum. Et ideo praedicamentale ens esse non potest nec relatio praedicamentalis, licet possit esse relatio secundum esse [inquantum relatio sic considerata] pure relatio est et non aliquid absolutum importat".

Chapter 2

Foundations in Nature
for the Semiotic Point of View

A point of view requires or presupposes a "standpoint"; and, if it is truly new, as is the case with semiotics, it normally requires some adjustments of terminology in order to be properly expressed, at least by revising the sense of existing terms, usually supplemented by the revival from desuetude of some obsolete terms, and sometimes too by the coining of new terms. This last option, however, should be considered a last resort, since it requires the utmost parsimony to be exercised with effectiveness. In what follows, I shall keep as far as possible to existing terms, adjusting their sense only through governing their use by the requirements which arise strictly with a view to the perspective grounded in the consideration of the action and being proper to signs.

Let us call the species-specifically distinct dimension or form of awareness proper to humans "understanding"; let us call the dimension of awareness generically common to human beings and other animals "perception"; and let us call the dimension of awareness out of which perception arises in the brute interactions between organisms and the physical environment "sensation". In laying down these procedural definitions, we are not begging the question as to what the difference between understanding and perception is, nor even the question of whether there is such a thing as a difference between understanding and perception. For we have already noted *that* and will shortly further see *why* every biological organism has a species-specifically distinct form or mode of awareness. And the question as to what that species-specifically distinct mode is in any given case is one that can be resolved only by a combination of observation and reflective analysis. How do horses perceive the world differently from dogs, and dogs from crocodiles, bees from gila monsters, and so on? We can in each case speak of "equine intelligence", "canine intelligence", "crocodilian intelligence", "apiarian intelligence", "gilan intelligence", and so on. So also with our use of understanding to designate species-specifically human intelligence: the designation does not beg any question, but simply provides a marker under which our answer to the specific question can be identified, whether affirmatively or negatively.

As a kind of general *obiter dictum*, let me add some substantive remarks here on the rather surprising novelty, that is to say, newness, of the semiotic point of view. A point of view, after all, is simply a unified way of looking at things. It constitutes formally the unity of what it objectifies. To "adopt a point of view" is to do nothing more than thematically to objectify in a definite way. A human being looked at "from the atomic point of view" appears no differently than does a stone or an alligator or any other object so regarded: the point of view is what determines the possible results of an enquiry, regardless of further differences in the objects viewed taken in their subjective being which might require yet other points of view to be brought effectively into consideration or to be accounted for fully and adequately. A point of view, moreover, may either find unity or create unity: the atomic structure is there in all bodies to be regarded; quantity is there in all bodies enabling the application of mathematics to the physical environment; but a conspiracy buff sees conspiracies where

>17<

they are and where they are not indifferently; a paranoid finds enemies even where they do not exist; and so on.

What about the semiotic point of view? Does it find unity or make unity across its objective field? Is the standpoint from which it arises a creation of the mind alone, or does the mind in achieving this standpoint have some assistance and collusion with the physical world itself in what it has prejacently to the involvement of human understanding? Is semiotics, assuredly a creature of mind, in the full scope of its possibilities and ground, a creature of mind alone, or does it have a foundation which gives the action of signs a footing on both sides of the divide between reveries of thought and the brute secondness of nature in its material and physical being?

The question is hardly empty, though it is only as old as Augustine. One of the really surprising things about semiotics, it strikes me, is the fact that the possibility of a unified object for its investigation does not seem to have been realized before the time of Augustine, in whose works, according to those who should know,[1] we encounter for the first time the general idea of the sign as applicable equally to natural phenomena like clouds and cultural phenomena like words or buttons.

But is this idea merely an invention on Augustine's part, perhaps like Oliver Stone's movie on the assassination of JFK, or does Augustine succeed by expressing in this idea something that is also prejacent to the idea, a feature of or structure within the environment which, though by Augustine for the first time signified and so "made objective", yet was operative in the physical universe prior to Augustine's labeling of it with the Latin term *signum*?

As old as Augustine, the question is also as recent as Scruton, who, in a comment on some work of Umberto Eco,[2] with a tone so dripping scorn as clearly to convey by the very question the response Scruton haughtily (and ignorantly)

---

[1] I.e., those who have investigated the matter with a pretense to Greek along with Latin, namely, Eco and his students. See Eco *et al.* 1986; Manetti 1993.

[2] Scruton 1980. See the response of Eco 1984.

deemed correct, pointedly inquired how could there be a science of structures as diverse as buttons and clouds?

Augustine, to be sure, lacked Scruton's semiotic callowness; yet Augustine, being unlearned in Greek, seems not to have realized fully either the novelty of his proposal that there can be a unified notion of *signum* applying to natural and cultural phenomena alike, or the possibility of justifying and grounding such a proposal in terms of any structure of reality independent of the mind. For the mind indeed is the principal beneficiary and consumer of signs. Might it not also be the omnipotent sign maker? If the entrails of an animal can foretell the outcome of battle and the coincidence of stellar order at birth can foretell fate and character, surely anything can be made a sign. There is hardly need to root the structure of signification in anything other than mind!

That, however, is not the question. The question is not whether the mind can make a sign out of anything, but how a sign is in the first place possible? When the mind makes a sign, what is it that it does? Or when the mind finds a sign, as when the weather forecasters raised for the mission control of Apollo 13 the threat of a typhoon in the prime recovery zone, what is it that the mind finds? More generally, when semiotics arises as the knowledge derived from the study of the action of signs, what is it that semiotics expresses?

The first one successfully to answer the question posed by the idea of *signum* as Augustine proposed it at the end of the fourth century (the first one successfully to address what Augustine's formulation took for granted) was John Poinsot early in the seventeenth century. That is to say, Poinsot was the first thinker successfully to answer precisely the question of *how* there can be something in common between inferences from natural phenomena and inferences from cultural phenomena. In providing an answer to the question of what natural and cultural phenomena have in common as signs, moreover, he at the same time answered the question of how error is possible in both cases, and at the same time, inadvertently, truth. This is no small achievement. It bears examining in detail. We should be able to find again today the trail that leads from the origin of semiosis in nature to the culmination of semiosis in thought, and to mark along the way the principal plateaus or levels upon which semiosis achieves its results.

The fact that the dominant system of speculative philosophy in Poinsot's time was the Aristotelian physics as refined and ramified by the Latin scholastics after the time of Abelard (1079–1144) makes his semiotic thought difficult to access, and no doubt contributed heavily to the failure of his successors to realize the novelty of his doctrine of signs over the next three hundred years. The first glimpse of Poinsot's semiotic outside his Latin context came with the work of Jacques Maritain in the 1930s.[3] This work was followed up first by Herculano de Carvalho,[4] then by me,[5] and more recently by a growing list of scholars.[6] But enough underbrush has been cleared to enable us at this historical moment to move with comparative ease

[3] Full discussion of Maritain's role in the discovery of Poinsot's semiotic is provided in Deely 1986a, with added details in Sebeok 1989.

[4] Herculano de Carvalho 1967, 1969, 1970.

[5] See, in Deely 1988, the discussion of reviews of the 1985 Deely edition of Poinsot 1632.

[6] In 1994–1995, there were two Special Issues of journals dedicated to articles on the work of Poinsot: the John Poinsot Special Issue of the newly renamed *New Scholasticism* LXVIII (Summer 1994), with articles by Beuchot, Cahalan, Coombs, Doyle, Guagliardo, Raposa, Rasmussen, and Wells (see Deely Ed. 1994); and the John Poinsot Issue of *The Thomist* 58.4 (October 1994), commemorating the 350th anniversary of Poinsot's death with articles by Deely, Murphy, and Kronen. Articles on Poinsot appeared also in *Listening* and *The Modern Schoolman*, respectively, by Deely 1995 and Dalcourt 1994.

A 1995 monograph by Furton continued the expansion of the literature; but, on close examination, the title of this work, *A Medieval Semiotic*, proves more accurate than its subtitle, *Reference and Representation in John of St. Thomas' Theory of Signs*. Wherever Poinsot's doctrine of signs exceeds the requirements of Furton's preoccupation with "realism" in the sense of the 19th century Thomistic revival, Furton forces the text back to a standpoint based on the medieval way of distinguishing simply between logic as concerned with *ens rationis* and physics as concerned with *ens reale*, which, from Poinsot's point of view, is actually presemiotic. The "medieval semiotic" Furton presents is closer to the views of Roger Bacon (cf. Bacon

along a trail that until recently lay hidden in a thicket of semiotically arcane and misleading considerations.

The centerpiece in the system conceived originally otherwise than semiotically was the notion of substance in the sense discussed above, namely, the notion of the individual as a relative center of unity dependent from first to last on a network of environmental relations without which it could neither come to be in the first place nor continue to be once brought into existence. Yet this notion, sharply in contrast with the notion of "substance" which won the field of modern philosophy, is a fundamentally experiential notion, pragmaticistically compatible with the requirements that adoption of a semiotic point of view in experience would reveal in contrasting, from within objectivity, the action of signs as rooted sometimes in dimensions of the objective world which are purely such and other times in dimensions of the objective world manifestative of a physical substantiality part and parcel with the objectivity itself signified at the foundation or terminus of certain sign relations and networks of sign relations. Recognition of such a contrast, after all, is but an extension of the experience of the contrast between signs which exhibit in their objective representation (their significates) grounds for holding that they have roots in the physical environment in its aspect of indifference to our interests and concerns (such as smoke taken as a sign of burning), and signs which exhibit in their objective representation grounds for holding rather that they have no roots in the physical environment except through the medium of human interests and concerns (such as a flag taken as a sign of a certain country).

c.1267), with whose text Furton shows no familiarity, than to the views of John of St. Thomas *né* Poinsot.

Mention must be made also of the work of Maroosis treating Poinsot, as did also Raposa, in an explicitly Peircean context (Maroosis 1981, 1993); of other work of James Murphy (1990, 1991, 1994); and of the exceptionally promising work of Vincent Guagliardo (1992, 1993, 1994, 1995), whose premature death on August 13 of 1995 was a great loss to the developing understanding of the doctrine of signs. He was the only one at this time teaching semiotics at the Berkeley Graduate Theological Union.

As a result of this, so to say, semiotic compatibility of the context within which he was so thoroughly steeped, a thinker such as Poinsot, once his attention had been caught by the singularity of semiosis in being able to transpire with apparently equal facility in cases where the object signified did and did not have as such (in what is proper to it as this or that object) any correlate dimension of physicality, found at his disposal for achieving a demarcation of the standpoint from which such a singularity could be viewed in its irreducible propriety the material necessary to fashion conceptual tools requisite to achieve, express, and begin the development of a semiotic point of view, a point of view, as I noted for the purpose of writing *Introducing Semiotic*, with no paradigm of philosophy given in advance – a development of human understanding without precedent:[7]

> Beginning with the sign, that is, from the function of signs in our experience taken in their own right (semiosis), it is the task of semiotic to create a new paradigm – its own – and to review, criticize, and correct so far as possible all previous accounts of experience in the terms of *that* paradigm.

A new beginning.

The decisive insight for establishing the standpoint required and opening up the way of signs came from the realization on Poinsot's part that the proper contrast to consider in our experience of the environment is not that between private consciousness and reality supposed prejacent, but that between existing subjects, conscious or not, and the networks of relations between them, the two-way dependencies which contrast with the situation of subjective existence (and, at the same time, sustain its possibility) and presuppose (either as maintaining or being maintained by) that situation, but cannot be reduced to it.[8] For example, sea life requires, among

---

[7] Deely 1982: 3.

[8] The modern way of ideas, by contrast, was arrived at by contrasting the perspective of the observer, the psyche of the individual thinker, as "subjective", with the "objective" situation of nature as it might be

many things, water in the liquid state; and water requires, among other things, a planet with a surface in a certain temperature range. Given these, sea life becomes possible. But a given sea life organism or network of sea life organisms requires as well an internal structure. At the moment that this combination of external and internal structural conditions is realized, a given individual comes into being (the Latins called this moment "generation"); at the moment that this combination – on either or both sides – ceases, a given individual ceases to be (the Latins called this moment "corruption"). Generation and corruption take place in an instant, whereas the life of the organism takes place in time, as do the changes in the systems which first make possible and then finally impossible the continued existence of the individual substance.

The substance thus is a relative center of unity and action, and through its action it struggles so to dominate both the internal systemic requirements and the external environmental structures as to maintain itself in existence. At this effort the individual organism eventually fails, though often enough not before handing on the torch of life to offspring. Very late in the Latin development some thinkers came to call substance a *transcendental relation* or *transcendental relative being*. The qualification "transcendental" in the expressions is intended to make the point that a substance rises above the internal and external networks of relations upon which it at every moment depends insofar as it forms a unified center of action and being in its own right. The qualification "relation" is, strictly speaking, an overstatement,[9] intended, as is the

supposed to be independently of any such perspective. Out of this poorly drawn contrast between subjective and objective as point of departure, compounded by the failure to distinguish between representation as such and signification, arose all the paradoxes and antinomies of modern philosophy in its epistemological development and transformation into idealism.

9 Cahalan (1975, cited in Deely 1985: 474n116), speaking with the advantage of seeing where the discussion ultimately led, remarks sympathetically that "to say that transcendental relations are relative but not relations seems to be precisely the kind of paradox that the imperfect abstraction of analogical concepts accounts for"

more exact alternative expression "relative being", to make the point that the dominance of a substance over the external and internal sustaining network is never strictly absolute (never permanently secure) but always in the nature of a balancing act[10] with no possibility of a safety net, so that one mis-

(cf. Cahalan 1970). A contemporary observer of the developing discussion in the late 13th century, anonymous, but tentatively identified by Krempel (1952: 412–413; see also 250) as Bernard d'Auvergne, saw nothing good in terminology so equivocal, adoption of which he considered proof positive of gross ignorance: dicere "quod est duplex relatio, scilicet relatio secundum esse, et relatio secundum dici . . . est supra modum nescienter dictum", which Krempel approvingly paraphrases thus: "Quiconque parle d'une *relatio secundum dici* fait preuve d'une grossière ignorance". See note 13, p. 26 below.

[10] *Tractatus de Signis*, Second Preamble, Article 2, 89/41–47, and 90/3–6, 15–27: "things relative according to the way they must be expressed in discourse bear on a terminus rather by founding a relation than by actually respecting, and for that reason they do not respect the terminus in question in the rationale of a pure terminus, but according to some other rationale – that of a cause, say, or of an effect, or of an object, or of some such. . . . the principal significate of an expression expressing a relation according to the way a subject must be expressed in discourse is not a relation, but something else, upon which a relation follows. . . . The establishing of this difference also establishes that an expression expressing a transcendental relation – which is nothing else than a relation according to the way subjective being must be expressed in discourse – does not convey relation from its principal significate, but something absolute, upon which some relation follows or could follow. For if it does not convey an absolute, it will not be transcendental, that is, ranging through diverse categories, but will look to one category only. Whence a transcendental relation is not a form adventitious to a subject or absolute thing, but one assimilated to it, yet connoting something extrinsic upon which the subject depends or with which it is engaged, . . ". – "Relativa secundum dici potius erga terminum se habent fundando relationem quam actu respiciendo, et ideo non in ratione puri termini ipsum respiciunt, sed secundum aliam rationem, puta causae vel effectus aut obiecti aut quid simile. . . . Principale significatum relationis secundum dici non est relatio, sed aliquid aliud, ad quod sequitur relatio. . . . Ex quo etiam constat, quod relatio transcendentalis, quae non est alia a relatione secundum dici, non importat ex principali significato relationem, sed aliquid absolutum, ad quod sequitur vel sequi potest aliqua relatio. Nam si absolutum non importat, transcendentalis non erit, id est vagans per diversa genera, sed ad unum

step or one fatal intrusion into the balanced systems – sooner or later inevitable – always proves fatal.

As an historical aside here, we may observe that this late Latin use of the term "transcendental" to modify the notion of relative being became, in effect, detached and separated from its modification and simply absolutized in the German phase of the classical modern development of philosophy after Descartes.[11] Kant in particular turned the term "transcendental" to the expression of a theme of philosophy's utter abandonment of any notion of relativity not created by the working of the understanding alone.[12] This abandonment, in effect, foreclosed the possibility of semiotic by precluding the foundational understanding of the sign as a vehicle of communication which transcends the divide between what exists from physical nature and what exists from the activity of finite mind, and does so by consisting in a triadic relation indifferent to its interpretant being mental.

Yet it cannot be thought that the Latins themselves were blameless in the matter of the use to which the term *transcendentalis* was eventually put by the moderns; for the Latins themselves, even when they meant only a relative independence of possible existence, had spoken most commonly of substance as an *absolute* being in contrast to that feeblest of being (*"ens minimum"*), relation considered purely and strictly as such (*"relatio secundum esse"*). The tardy introduction of the qualification of this earlier and more common way of speaking of substance as *ens absolutum* by an expression intended to make explicit what had been implicit all along by manifesting that *"imbibita rei absolutae"* – i.e., part and parcel with the somewhat misleadingly so-called "absolute being" – was the reality and notion of a network of dependencies in which the independence of substance was itself relativized

---

praedicamentum tantum spectabit. Unde relatio transcendentalis non est forma adveniens subiecto seu rei absolutae, sed illi imbibita, connotans tamen aliquid extrinsecum, a quo pendet vel circa quod versatur, . . .".

11 See Doyle 1997.

12 See Ch. 5, note 15, p. 59 below.

came, we may say, as too little too late to stem the tide of classical modernity.[13] The mainstream early moderns who begot especially rationalism took no notice of this later discussion among the Latins. They simply appropriated to the framework of their radically unsemiotic epistemological paradigm the use both of the term "substance" and of the term "transcendental". Today, so late in the game, indeed, the very attempt to retrieve these terms for semiotic – markers among others of the divide in history between the end of the Latin Age and the onset of modernity – would be best left to Don Quixote, were it not for the fact that the paradigm shift semiotics imposes upon epistemology, natural philosophy, and philosophy of science alike is congenial to the earlier while incompatible with the later usage of both these terms in philosophy.

For in contrast to this substance as the relative center of unity and action are the *networks themselves*, both internal and external, on which the substance at all times depends. How are we to contrast the substance with the manner of its dependency on its surroundings, the physical environment in general? The question is important, for in this contrast Poinsot was able to uncover and divine the feature of nature which makes the being of signs possible in the first place – the indifference, as we shall see, of relation to its subjective ground.

The dependency of substance on physical environment is maintained only indirectly through anything pertaining to the substance in its subjective unity as a relative being.[14] Directly

---

[13] Krempel (1952: 670), who, if he understands modernity, understands little else, bemoans "cette relation transcendentale, à la fois réelle et identique à l'absolu créé", as "la déviation la plus tragique de la scolastique décadente". His massive study of this area, thus concluded, is invaluable for its collection of texts but obtuse in its analysis of them (see the notes on Krempel in the 1985 edition of Poinsot 1632). By his collection of the texts, however, even ignoring his theoretical analyses, which are generally suspect, it seems possible to date the terminology as we have basically discussed it to the 16th century (see esp. Ch. XVIII and the Appendix in Krempel's work); and he is certainly right in his characterization of Poinsot (p. 669) as the "vrai théoricien" of this discussion, even though his reasoning about the whole matter is hopeless.

[14] *Tractatus de Signis*, Second Preamble, Article 2, 90/23–27: "Whence a

it is maintained precisely through the multiplicity of *connections between* that unity and the varieties of other such unities which constitute other substances and, in their totality, as including both their actions and interactions (their mutual dependencies), the physical universe or "cosmos" as a whole, a totality of individuals and places which itself has no place (because it has no surroundings). Looked at in themselves, the relative unities are substances, beings in their own right which depend upon others and upon which others depend. As beings in their own right the substances have a *subjective constitution and structure* which distinguishes them both from that upon which they depend and from that which depends upon them. But the two-way dependencies which contrast with this situation of subjective existence (and, at the same time, sustain its possibility) and presuppose (either as maintaining or being maintained by) it have no such being in themselves. Their "constitution", if we may so speak in the case, is wholly external to the beings maintained and maintaining.[15] If we are

> transcendental relation is not a form adventitious to a subject or absolute thing, but one assimilated to it, yet connoting something extrinsic upon which the subject depends or with which it is engaged" – "Unde relatio transcendentalis non est forma adveniens subiecto seu rei absolutae, sed illi imbibita, connotans tamen aliquid extrinsecum, a quo pendet vel circa quod versatur".

15 *Tractatus de Signis*, Second Preamble, Article 2, 89/7–20: "in the *Summa Theologica*, I, q. 28, art. 1, [St. Thomas] says that 'those things which are said to be toward something signify, according to their proper rationale only a respect toward another. This respect sometimes indeed is in the nature of things, as when some things are ordered among themselves according to their nature. And the reason for this is that relation, on account of its minimal entitative character, does not depend on a subject in precisely the same way as the other absolute forms, but stands rather as a third kind of being consisting in and resulting from the coordination [in time] of two extremes; and therefore, in order to exist in the nature of things, a relation continuously depends on the fundament coordinating it with a term, and not only on a subject and productive cause". – "in 1. p. q. 28. art. 1. [D. Thomas] inquit, quod 'ea, quae dicuntur ad aliquid, significant secundum propriam rationem solum respectum ad aliud. Qui quidem respectus aliquando est in rerum natura, utpote quando aliquae res secundum naturam suam ad invicem ordinatae sunt.' Et hoc ideo

to say that the being maintained, the substance, has a subjective existence, then we must say by contrast that the maintained and maintaining "beings" are entirely *intersubjective*, having whatever further "nature" they have but indirectly, through the respective properties (or "accidents") of substances which they maintain or by which they are maintained.[16]

> est, quia relatio propter suam minimam entitatem non praecise dependet a subiecto sicut aliae formae absolutae, sed se habet ut entitas tertia ex coordinatione duorum extremorum consistens et resultans, ideoque ut sit in rerum natura debet dependere a fundamento coordinante illam ad terminum, et non solum a subiecto et causa productiva". See also 82/7–18 and 86/6–22.

[16] *Tractatus de Signis*, Second Preamble, Article 2, 99/23–42: "But the fact that a categorial relation is said to be in a subject does not take away from the fact that its whole being is toward another – 'whole', I say, that is, the being proper and peculiar to itself, in which it differs from other absolute categories or subjective kinds of being; yet by supposing the common rationale of an accident, namely, to be in something, by reason of which rationale an accident does not have to be toward another, but does not exclude it either.

"[A] transcendental relation is not primarily and essentially toward another, as has been said, but from another or concerning another, as a dependency or a causality or something of the kind; which can sometimes be verified not by that which is the case in fact but by that which could be the case or that which is required for something's being the case. But a categorial relation, because it has its whole being toward another, does not arise except from the positing in fact of the extremes. Whence if either is lacking, the categorial relation itself ceases to be".

"Quod vero relatio praedicamentalis dicitur esse in subiecto, non tollit, quin totum suum esse sit ad aliud, totum, inquam, id est proprium et peculiare ipsius esse, in quo differt ab aliis generibus absolutis; supponendo tamen rationem communem accidentis, scilicet esse in aliquo, ratione cuius non habet esse ad aliud, sed nec id excludit.

"[T]ranscendentalis relatio non est primo et per se ad aliud, ut dictum est, sed ab alio vel circa aliud, ut dependentia vel causalitas aut aliquid simile; quod aliquando salvari potest non per id, quod de facto est sed per id, quod convenire potest, vel postulat, ut conveniat. Relatio autem praedicamentalis, quia totum suum esse habet ad aliud, non consurgit nisi ex positione extremorum. Unde altero illorum deficiente deficit".

See also Powell 1983, 1986.

Remember that the context of the discussion thus far, lacking the name, is nonetheless thoroughly pragmaticistic, being entirely that of the physical environment distinguished within the objective world of experience as that common dimension of sense-perceptible objects which does not reduce to our experience of them. It is not a question of cognitive organisms, specifically, nor even of organisms as such, but of the requirements of a world consisting of "a many of which each is one" – Aristotle's famous answer to the ancient question of "whether the world is one or many".[17] Hence the intersubjective component spoken of is a question initially of physical existence and being, not yet a question of the semiosis of cognition, which yet remains presupposed and unthematized as such. The substances, as relative absolutes, depend upon absolute relatives,[18] which are intersubjective components of the environmental situation within and upon which the subjective centers of being and action depend even while providing their foundations and termini. These intersubjective components as such the Latins called *pure relations*, but more specifically "categorial" or *physical relations*, insofar as it was not yet a question of anything existing outside the order of physical being as constituting the world of nature according to its own possibilities independent of human existence and experience alike.[19]

[17] For a detailed spelling out from a standpoint of Latin Scholastic natural philosophy, see Deely 1969, and Ashley 1973.

[18] In my graduate school days, the joke among students on this point was as follows: so the whole of physical reality can be divided into three types of being: relative absolutes, or substances; absolute relatives, or relations; and absolute absolutes, which is restricted to *Deus et alia huiusmodi* – God and other things of the kind (such as the rationalist substances!): the point of the joke being that there are no "other things of this kind".

[19] In Latin parlance, anything of the physical order was commonly designated as "categorial being" or *ens reale*. By a series of unfortunate translations which continue to haunt and bedevil philosophical discussion today, modern authors outside the Latin came to speak of this physical order of being as the "real world" or "reality". But the expression *ens reale* in Latin times in fact gave voice to a cultural preoccupation, and not to an exclusive notion but to an oppositional one

It was a question neither of signs nor of minds, even though both were at work in determining what it *was* a question of: the basic nature of the physical world.

Now among the substances, some are living and some seem not to be. Every substance is such by reason of having, as its material correlate, a form: *forma dat esse*. But, to distinguish the case of substances clearly living, the form in that case they called *soul* (or *anima*), whence we get our notion of "animation" in its variety of senses. Along with soul enters the possibility of mind, "mind" being nothing more than an expression to designate those souls capable of cognition – "animals" in contrast to "plants".

When mind enters in, what does it do? To begin with, it constitutes certain aspects of the physical environment – those to which the cognitive powers of the animal organism are proportioned and (especially) in which it has a vital interest (as predator or prey, say) – as *objects* of apprehension. "Mind" in its most rudimentary function simply relates the cognitive organism apprehensively to what the organism itself is not but upon which it vitally depends, namely, various aspects of the physical surroundings,[20] and adds to those aspects but a

(see the discussion of the point in Deely 1985: 465–67, esp. 466n107); for, in their reflective and critical moments, the Latins – at least the better among their philosophers – well recognized that the world of culture even taken *as such* is no less "real" than the world of nature of which culture is both complement and part. But this is another story, the beginning of which can be found in the diagram "Divisions of being in the structure of experience" in Deely 1982: 26, and the moral of which is well made in the conclusion of Sebeok 1984.

20 *Tractatus de Signis*, Second Preamble, Article 2, 99/6–23: "the entire specific rationale and essence of transcendental relations derives from or depends on another. . . . For example . . . cognitive acts depend on an object, as upon causes from which they have existence and specification. . . . And for this reason it is said that . . . [it is] as from another or concerning another or by any other mode of causality whatever [that] a transcendental relation respects a terminus . . ". – "relatio transcendentalis . . . tota earum species et essentia sumatur ab alio vel dependeat ab alio, . . . sicut . . . dependet . . . actus ab obiecto sicut a causis, a quibus habent esse et specificationem. . . . Et ideo dicitur, quod respicit terminum . . . ut ab alio vel circa aliud vel quocumque alio causalitatis modo". The reader is well invited to ponder *in situ* this tortured ellipsis.

relation to the organism as cognizing.[21] Mind in its origins *objectifies something of the prejacent physical* surrounding the cognitive substance. Since the organism, as we have seen, is from the first enmeshed in a whole intersubjective complex of physical relationships (we might well picture this complex as a web and the organism as the spider which spun the web and waits at its center for what the web will catch[22]), the first thing that "mind" does is simply allow the organism to be aware of certain of those intersubjective relationships in which it is caught up, particularly the ones at whose terminus lies food (or, in the case of motile organisms, danger). "Mind" does no

[21] Whence it is said that the cognitive capacities or 'mind' of an organism, as an inherent attribute or characteristic of an organism, is a subjective possession or feature, a part of the subjectivity of the organism as a substantial whole, but one which *serves to create or found* suprasubjective connections between that organism and its environment, both physical and objective. Like the organism itself which requires, to be understood, to be thought in terms of the environment on which it depends, so the cognitive aspect of the organism, to be understood, has to be thought in terms of what it can objectify. The organism is not what it depends upon, any more than a cognitive power is what it objectifies; but outside the context of those correlates neither the one nor the other can be fully understood. So the *Tractatus de Signis*, Second Preamble, Article 2, 90/15–20: "The establishing of this difference also establishes that a transcendental relation – which is nothing else than a relation according to the way subjective being must be expressed in discourse – conveys from its principal significate not a relation, but something absolute, upon which some relation *follows or could follow*". – "Ex quo etiam constat, quod relatio transcendentalis, quae non est alia a relatione secundum dici, non importat ex principali significato relationem, sed aliquid absolutum, ad quod *sequitur vel sequi potest* aliqua relatio". To be relative *secundum dici* – according to the requirements of being understood, or discursively expressed – and to be something absolute, a subject or a subjective modification of being, considered as founding or able to found a relation (which also happens in terminating a reciprocal relation) *secundum esse*, is the same thing. This is the point.

[22] This indeed was one of Jakob von Uexküll's core metaphors (1934: 14) in his development of the idea of Umwelt: "As the spider spins its threads, every subject spins his relations to certain characters of the things around him, and weaves them into a firm web which carries his existence". Cf. Deely 1994a: 218–22, which turns this metaphor into the three dimensions of a sphere of irregular surface.

more than provide the organism with a partial map to facilitate its survival in the physical world. This is the rudimentary sense of the semiotic term *Innenwelt*.

But mind soon does more than passively register some part of the organism's surroundings. There is more to mind than pure or simple *sensation* (defined by the Latins as the *actio sensibilis in sensu*, where "sensibilis" means the proportioned aspects of the substances constituting the physical environment). Mind takes an interest in what is there according to the preferences of the substance of which it is a dimension. These preferences are initially determined by the organism's biological heritage or nature. For what is different between food for a dragonfly and food for a dragon, beyond the difference between a real and mythical animal? The same as the difference between food for a cow and food for a dog, food for a lion and food for a mouse: the biological constitution of each animal determines what, in the whole range of physical surroundings, will provide nourishment and what will not, just as the biological constitution of each animal determines what, in the whole range of physical surroundings, will constitute a threat to the animal and what will not. At this moment the mind begins to *interpret* what the senses reveal. Here is the beginning of perception in its difference from sensation.

Chapter 3

The Semiosis of Sensation

But let us not pass too swiftly; we have so far said nothing at all about semiosis. Yet semiosis is already explicitly at work in the giving to sensations of a structure jointly determined by the physical nature of the termini of the relations of sensation and the physical nature of the organs of sense founding those relations. For simplicity's sake, let our example be that of an animal, one human or near to the human in evolutionary ascent, that is to say, let us use the case of an animal with the basic external sense powers of sight, hearing, smell, taste, and touch.

To each such power there corresponds an object: differentiated light or "color", sound, odors, flavors, and relative warmth or cold as radiating from a source which, if its temperature is not too extreme, will also yield to touch a texture. Yet given along with each such objective aspect of the physical world, and dependently thereon, there are also given movements, positions, numbers, sizes, distances. I have no intention here of reopening and entering again[1] upon the

---

[1] I say "again," because I have already reviewed the details of these traditional controversies in Deely 1994a: 73–88, and Deely 2001, ch. 12.

hoary controversies over so-called "primary" vs. "secondary" qualities and the rest. My interest is purely semiotic, and therefore I note simply that, wherever one thing is known on the basis of something else known, we are in the presence of the sign function. Even at its most rudimentary and simple beginnings, mind finds itself caught up in a series of relationships which reflection recognizes as semiotic relations, even though they are a set of relations that is physical, indeed, and naturally determined or, rather, codetermined by the biological constitution of the organism with its sensory apparatus on one side and the material structures of the environment on the other side.

It is enough to realize that the sensations an organism experiences at the core of perceptions exist *in between* these two structures of subjectivity (the individual constitution of the organism knowing and the material constitution of the environmental aspects of which the organism becomes aware) to see that the question of whether the sense qualities belong to mind or to object is nugatory. They belong to the interaction of organism and physical environment insofar as that interaction falls within the range of the organism's cognitive sensibilities or "powers", providing a purchase, first, for whatever type of organism, to survive; but further, for organisms such as our own, to develop theoretical investigations in either direction – the direction of mind with its underlying nature, or the direction of physical environment in *its* underlying nature (or natures).

The "purpose" of sensation, if we may so loosely speak, is to reveal not any "world in itself" but what the environmental situation is *so far as the cognitive organism is involved* – a world, if you like, of "participant apprehension". This the Latins well understood, as is clear from their formula: *sensatio est actio sensibilis in sensu*. Analytically prescissed and strictly taken, sensation reveals an aspect of passivity wherein mind is open to, dependent upon, and even, as it were, at the mercy of specific elements within the physical ambience wherein it exists. So far as sensation reveals a passive dimension or *aspect* of awareness, however, sensation also reveals a primitive network

>34<

of relations which are physical as well as cognitive *at one and the same time*. Considered in its own right and prescissively as such, sensation reveals a network in which the reticulates, veins, or strands are founded in a physical subject (the organism or substance) on the basis of modifications made upon it by the physical surroundings. And these same relations individually terminate in the environmental source of those modifications precisely by revealing and inasmuch as they reveal some proportion obtaining here and now in the interaction between organism and environment[2] whereby the two are linked in a cognition or awareness which is at the same time a physical relationship (a reticle, as it were) involving the physical being of environment and environed mutually entangled as here and now coexisting. This abduction finds its suggestive ground (and, in the end, its inductive verification) in the fact that the right type of organism (such as our own) is therewith – i.e., in and by sensation – given the possibility of discovering *also* aspects of so-called cause and effect. These are but the discoverable dependencies of one environmental factor, aspect, or influence upon another in the formation of a change which would lead an infinite intelligence at once to an understanding of the universe as an interactive whole. They lead a finite discursive intelligence toward exactly the same point, but only asymptotically and in function of the gradual formation of an ever growing community of inquirers whose language[3] preserves their investigative results and so comes

---

[2] Cf. *Tractatus de Signis*, Second Preamble, Article 2, 90/41–91/28.

[3] That the project of human understanding must finally be an achievement of community to which individuals but contribute (dependent upon their language as the symbolic growth sufficiently capable of preserving past achievements to communicate them culturally with relative independence of socially living groups, as I would put it – see Deely 1992) is a sentiment nicely expressed by Will Durant in a passing comment on Roman sculpture (1944: 350): "The greatest of the portrait busts is the so-named Head of Caesar, of black basalt, in Berlin. . . . Only second to it is the colossal head of Caesar in Naples; here the wrinkles have set almost into bitterness, as if the giant had at last discovered that no mind is broad enough to understand, much less to rule, the world".

to sustain over time that kind of intelligence which we label, for want of a better term, "scientific".

This fundamental point about the sensory core of perception as providing a purchase alike for survival and for investigation could hardly better be made than in the following quotation from a work of the French geneticist, François Jacob:[4]

> No matter how an organism investigates its environment, the perception it gets must necessarily reflect so-called "reality" and, more specifically, those aspects of reality which are directly related to its own behavior. If the image that a bird gets of the insects it needs to feed its progeny does not reflect at least some aspects of reality, there are no more progeny. If the representation that a monkey builds of the branch it wants to leap to has nothing to do with reality, then there is no more monkey. And if this did not apply to ourselves, we would not be here to discuss this point.

Since we are here to discuss the point, let us move on to the further point that the making present in cognition of one object or objective aspect of the environment by another fulfills the minimal sign function, all right, but it does not yet reveal what is distinctive about semiosis in its contrast with physical interactions. All that we have seen so far is that there are in sensation sign relations which are not the creations of mind, even though the mind as organ of apprehension depends in sense *perception* further upon sign relations which it itself makes, or to which it itself gives rise.

To begin to grasp what is distinctive about the action of signs we must move beyond sensation to consider the active aspect of the mind apprehending. We must look at the way sensation is incorporated into a larger objective whole – the case of perception in contrast to sensation prescissively considered – to create the world of experience (or Umwelt), which is proper to every organism in a fundamentally species-specific

4 Jacob 1982: 56.

way. In transcending its sensory core, the perceiving mind moves beyond the environment as prejacent physical surroundings objectified in sensation to a larger objective sphere which, in contrast with whatever organization belongs to the physical environment as such, and even though partially incorporating in its objectification that physical organization, receives from the perceiving itself an overall organization proper to itself. "Differences among physical things as such are one thing", Poinsot remarks laconically (echoing Cajetan from a hundred years before[5]), but "differences among objects as such are quite something else again".

---

[5] See Cajetan 1507: *In I Summam Theologicam*, q. 1. art. 3; and the *Tractatus de Signis*, Book I, Question 2, 149/44 (this text is cited in Ch. 6, note 26, p. 98 below), Question 4, 187/32, Book II, Question 1, 270/39; also Poinsot 1635, in Reiser 1937: 76b37–77b25, cited in the Deely edition of the *Tractatus* at 179/1 note 13.

Chapter 4

From Sensation to Umwelt
as Species-Specific Objective World

Take the case of any organism. What does it need in order to survive and thrive? This is a matter of interest to the organism alone (of considerable interest). The physical environment as such is supremely indifferent to such needs. It antecedes the organism and does just fine, thank you, in that specific organism's absence.[1] As a consequence, it is up to the organism not only to achieve a selective awareness of its environment in sensation, but to realign those elements according to its own interests and to add to them as necessary to achieve over the environment a sufficient transcendence to compel the environment, despite or against its prejacent indifference, to support the organism's own further development and well being.[2]

---

[1]   This is true synchronically, even though in the overall evolution of life there develops a reciprocity between organisms and environment through which the environment itself is modified diachronically in the direction of enabling new and ever higher forms in a mutual subsistence.

[2]   *Tractatus de Signis*, First Preamble, Article 1, 50/29–32 (repeated at 72/5–8): "a mind-dependent objective being or aspect thereof is

>38<

We enter into the domain of perception in its contrast with simple sensation as soon as begins this process – a twofold and correlative process, at once psychological in the *Innenwelt* and objective in the Umwelt – of *combining* environmental elements differently in cognition ("objectively") than they are combined in physical relationships obtaining prejacently to and independently of the organism and *adding* through cognition yet new relationships specifically based on the organism's needs and desires rather than on the action on the senses of prejacent physical structures of the ambient surroundings.[3] Simple partial awareness (or objectification) of immediate

produced whenever the understanding attempts to apprehend that which does not exist, and therefore construes that which is not as if it were a being" – "tunc efficitur ens rationis, quando intellectus nititur apprehendere, quod non est, et ideo fingit illud ac si esset ens". How these remarks, here framed explicitly in terms of understanding, apply also to perception in its proper mode and dimension of apprehension, Poinsot elsewhere makes explicit (68/17–31): "But that sense is able to know fictive being materially . . . is proved by this fact, that internal sense synthesizes many things which outside itself in no way are or can be. Sense therefore knows something which is in itself a constructed or fictive being, although the fiction itself sense does not apprehend, but only that which, in the fictive being, offers itself as sensible". – "Quod vero ens fictum materialiter possit cognoscere sensus . . . ex eo probatur, quia sensus internus multa ad invicem componit, quae extra se nullo modo sunt aut esse possunt. Cognoscit ergo aliquid, quod in se est ens fictum, licet ipsam fictionem non apprehendat, sed solum id, quod in illo ente ficto tamquam sensibile se offert". See Ch. 6, note 7, p. 72 ff. below for the conclusion to which this phenomenological appeal is added.

3   "We suppose that there are iconic specifications, or ideas, at work in perception, just as there is cognition there. For if perceptions are higher in the knowing process than are sensations, they also require higher forms of specification, or at least ones ordered in a higher way, in order to bring forth a higher level of awareness. But specifiers of a more perfect and elevated type are seen to be necessary particularly when the objects represented are of a more abstract character [i.e., more removed from the here-and-now immediacy of sensation], as is the case with such perceptible but unsensed characteristics as hatred, unfriendliness, offspring, parents, and so forth. For these formalities are not represented in the external senses, and yet they are known in perception; therefore there exists some principle representative of

physical surroundings is not enough; it is up to the organism to find and to get what it needs from the surroundings. To this end the organism must coat its sensations with interpretation not simply according to what *is* there but according to what the organism *wants and needs* to be there if it is to survive and thrive. This is the rationale for the semiotic notion of Umwelt as *a species-specific objective world*, a notion that so scandalized Roland Posner when I proposed it in these terms at the "Semiotics: Field or Discipline?" State-of-the-Art Conference organized by Michael Herzfeld at Indiana University's Bloomington campus in 1984.[4]

In creating through perception its species-specific objective world or Umwelt, the organism is, if anything, even more

them, which must not be so material and imperfect as to obtain at the level of the sensed objects as such, at which level the cognitions of external sense are constrained. Therefore it must be a form of specification more perfect than a specification of external sense, which represents only sensed [as contrasted to perceived] things" – "Supponimus dari species in sensibus internis, sicut datur cognitio. Quodsi illae potentiae internae sunt altiores in cognoscendo, etiam requirunt altiores species vel saltem altiori modo ordinatas, ut cognitio elevatior elici possit. Specialiter autem quando obiecta repraesentata sunt altioris abstractionis, ut intentiones insensatae, requirere videntur aliquas species perfectiores et elevatiores repraesentantes tales intentiones, sicut odium, inimicitiam, filios, parentes etc. Istae enim formalitates non repraesentantur in sensibus externis, et tamen cognoscuntur ab internis, ergo datur aliquod principium repraesentativum illarum, quod non debet esse ita materiale et imperfectum, quod sistat in ipsis rebus sensatis, sicut sistunt sensus externi; ergo perfectior species debet esse quam species sensus externi, quae solum repraesentat res sensatas" (from Poinsot 1635: 265b9–32, included in the 1985 Deely edition of the *Tractatus de Signis* as note 8 to Book II, Question 2, at 243/22; related text in Ch. 6, notes 2 and 12, pp. 69 and 81 f. below. See also note 27 to Book II, Question 2, at 249/20). Recent discussion in Beuchot 1991 and 1993: esp. 24–28.

4   See "Semiotic as Framework and Direction" (Deely 1984). Posner failed to account for (a failure in which he is hardly alone: cfr. Deely 1994: Gloss 2 on ¶9, p. 136) the specifically semiotic notion of objectivity that the sign, as that which every object presupposes, implies in order for semiosis to be possible in the first place in its distinctive role of mediating the physical and the objective in the achievement of thirdness.

"self-interested" than sensation. Sensation is already self-interested in that the subjectivity of the organism, the biological heritage of its physical constitution, is what determines the range of environmental stimuli it will be possible for the organism to become aware of through sensation. This self-interest present in sensation is magnified in perception. To continue the quotation of Jacob begun in the last chapter:[5]

> Perceiving certain aspects of reality is a biological necessity; certain aspects only, for obviously our perception of the external world is massively filtered. Our sensory equipment allows us to see a tiger entering our room, but not the cloud of particles which, according to physicists, constitutes the reality of a tiger.

Here the word "reality" should surely be put into quotation marks, for Jacob is unwittingly evincing the influence of the decidedly medieval and inadequate notion of reality – which modernity inherited unchanged – as the cognition-prejacent-and-independent aspects of the physical environment which has so muddied the discussion of mind for the three and a half centuries wherein classical modern philosophy eventually strangled itself in the coils of the misbegotten controversy between "realism" and "idealism". The death-rattle of this quintessentially modern debate sounds at the frontier where modernity finally gives way to postmodernity and the rise of semiotic consciousness.[6] Modern philosophy, in short, unwittingly committed itself to indefensible boundaries by combining a reductive and ultimately inadequate notion of reality with an epistemological paradigm in which was collapsed the difference between signification as such and the representative elements within signification which are not signs formally and strictly considered. These elements are only the foundational and fundamental elements, the sign-vehicles, on the basis of which the signs themselves, as relations as irreducibly suprasubjective and triadic, consurge in

[5] Jacob 1982: 56.
[6] See Deely 1994a, 1995, and 2001; Santaella-Braga 1994.

their proper being. The Durants[7] posed without answering an intriguing question – "Has all the progress of philosophy since Descartes been a mistake through its failure to recognize the role of myth in the consolation and control of man?" – to which semiotics decisively answers in the affirmative.

The cultural interpretant for the term "reality" in the background of Jacob's text aside, however, the central point clearly stands: the need for sensations at the core of perception to be in contact with the physical surroundings as incorporating those points of contact into the objective world (the world of which the organism is aware as the organism is aware of it). Also clear is the rationale why perception compounds this self-interest by adding to the naturally determined sign relations of sensation further relations of its own devising. These added relations may be one-sided and comparatively "unreal" from the imaginary standpoint of the prejacent physical surroundings; but they are equally "real" from the actual standpoint of relations as having a physical basis (in the physiological and psychological processes of the organism) and a physical term (in the aspects of the surroundings organized objectively to meet the organism's interests),[8] and they are equally triadic with the sign-relations of sensation in the making present *of* objects *to* the organism *on the basis* of that mediation between physical and objective being in which semiosis above all consists.

Thus, with perception, do deceit and cunning enter into the objective world, as well as territoriality and care for offspring and all the rest of the distinguishing behaviors of a species. Perception adds to sensation's web that flurry of further apprehensive strands that reticulate well beyond the immediate proportions of physical interaction verified in sensation to construct in its totality an objective world suited to the specific needs and interests of the perceiving lifeform:[9]

> The external world, the "reality" of which we all have
> intuitive knowledge, thus appears as a creation of the

[7]   Will and Ariel Durant 1968: 97.

[8]   See Ch. 6, note 12, p. 81 f. below.

[9]   Continuing again Jacob 1982: 56.

nervous system. It is, in a way, a possible world, a model allowing the organism to handle the bulk of incoming information and make it useful for its everyday life. One is thus led to define some kind of "biological reality" as the particular representation of the external world that the brain of a given species is able to build. The quality of such biological reality evolves with the nervous system in general and brain in particular.

Note again in Jacob's text the lurking of a cultural interpretant or bias in favor of the inadequate medieval and renaissance notion of "reality" commented on just above. The "external world" is but a part of the objective world; but, as external, it is hardly the creation of the subject's nervous system alone, but of that system in interaction with environmental influences on the sensory terminations of the central nervous system giving rise to that whole series of experiential relations at once physical and objective, as we have seen. This being said, and having also said that the "model world" through which each individual and species achieves such survival and thrival as it does has come to be called in semiotics the Umwelt or species-specific objective world, we need to insert at this point a caveat.

Even though the notion of model and modeling system is highly useful and, indeed, indispensable to understanding the semiotic *Innenwelt* correlated with the objective world, it yet cannot be used as fully equivalent to the notion itself of Umwelt. A number of considerations compel this conclusion, beginning with the fact that the "model world" in question is much more than a mere "creation of the nervous system" inasmuch as it necessarily includes, on Jacob's own accounting, necessary elements representing – "transcendentally representing" or "relative" in the late Latin terminology discussed above[10] – the physical environment on which the species is dependent for survival, and hence giving rise to those intersubjective connections which, as we have seen, give

---

[10] Ch. 2, esp. pp. 23–26.

physical reality to the suprasubjective being in which relations as such minimally and always consist. By emphasizing one-sidedly the role of the brain, Jacob gives vent to that same modern reductionism which so intrudes to mar the otherwise semiotically superb work of Paul Bouissac (and sometimes Sebeok).

The Umwelt is a "model world" from the point of view of possibility, one of the infinite variety of possible alternatives according to which the bare physical furnishings of the environment can be arranged and incorporated into an architectural superstructure of possible experiences, supposing especially this or that biological form.[11] But from the point of view of its inhabitants, an Umwelt is the actual world of experience and everyday reality, in comparison to which the prejacent physical in its proper being is secondary, derivative, and not necessarily recognized according to the intrinsic requirements of its own being at all. We think today, for example, generally, that a human Umwelt which incorporates the institution of slavery is a less acceptable species-specific habitat than one which is free of slavery. The "model world" of the twentieth century is sharply different in this regard from the "model world" acceptable to and inhabited by the ancient Greeks, Saint Paul, medieval man, etc.[12] The Umwelt of Sparta differed sharply from that of Athens, and much physical appropriation of physical resources within the shared environment was put to the use of determining which objective model should dominate over or even supplant the other. Rome sought to destroy not the physical lining of the Carthaginian Umwelt so much as the Umwelt itself as sustained by that lining. *Delenda est Carthago.*

This brings us directly to the main problem with the term "model" and "modeling system" as a proposed translation or 'synonym' for Umwelt. The notion of model often suggests a representation in miniature or in part of something else which is by comparison real. This connotation of the term "model" and "modeling system" applies to the Umwelt only insofar as

[11] I borrow here from ¶s 123, 127, and 128 of Deely 1994.
[12] See Deely 1996.

the objective world harbors virtually scientific theories in the specific sense proper to humans – i.e., in the most general terms, insofar as an objective world is anthroposemiotically as well as zoösemiotically constituted. The "model world" of the dragonfly is not primarily a representation of something else more real by comparison. To the extent that world contains – inevitably as we have noted with Jacob – elements representing as such physical aspects of the dragonfly's surroundings, these elements are not more real than the Umwelt itself but considerably less real, and derive their interest, moreover, specifically from their place in the larger objective whole which precisely does not at all points objectively correspond to physical elements in the surroundings. In this respect, the Umwelt of the dragonfly is not a model world, it is the real world, wherein the dragonfly lives and moves and has its being.

What has just been said of the dragonfly Umwelt holds as a general point. Only from an external point of view can we speak of an Umwelt in its totality – as distinct from the scientific enterprise subspecific to the human Umwelt – as a "modeling system". From within any given Umwelt, that Umwelt is the reality for the specific individual. It is not a model world, it is the objective world of experience, with respect to which physical being comprises only a part which may or may not be modeled in what is proper to it by any given construct of understanding. The notion of reality and the notion of the Umwelt are thus, from the point of view of experience, inseparable. What is distinctive about experience within the human Umwelt is, quite precisely, the notion that Umwelt and reality are yet not coextensive, any more than Umwelt and physical environment, or physical environment and reality, are coextensive. From this bare suspicion of the understanding in its difference from sense arises, on the one hand, morality as distinct from mores, and, on the other hand, the whole enterprise of science and technology, to say nothing of philosophy.

Hence the point is that, prescissively considered, it is not in sensation but in perception that the distinctiveness of the action of signs begins to reveal itself: what is, is put at the service of what is not yet. Whether virtually in a stone (the case of physiosemiosis) or in a plant (the case of phyto-semiosis), or actually in a cognitive organism (the case alike of zoösemiosis and of anthroposemiosis), the "ideal element", the "interpretant" linking sign to signified, regulative of action toward the future which is to be different from what simply is, enters into semiosis and is the reason for its triadicity.

Chapter 5

How Is the Distinctiveness
of Semiosis in General Possible?

Now how is this distinctive action of signs, whereby the cognizing organism transcends objectively the limits of its actual physical surroundings, possible?

Since the question has not previously been asked in these specific terms, it behooves us to begin with the only text that provides an answer to the question at least in its own terms.

According to the *Tractatus de Signis*, the whole process of sign action, no less in perception than in sensation (or, for that matter, in nature at large), is rooted in the feature which distinguishes pure relations already in their environmental inter-subjective manifestations from the subjectivity of substance, from all that distinguishes the individual according to its intrinsic constitution. This is the feature of relation according to which relation as suprasubjective is indifferent to the subjective foundation or ground according to which the relation arises now from physical nature or now from cognition, or indeed from both simultaneously.

Let us see how far this answer goes, and to what extent it can be improved upon.

In whatever case, a relation is able to be physical depending only on the circumstance external to the relation itself of whether the terminus of the relation, that to which the relation connects its subject (physical or objective), has a material correlate in the environment formally corresponding with its fundament, that aspect or characteristic of the subject which is the basis or ground from which the relation springs.

In the case where an "idea" is involved, this requires no more than a structure physically objective (physical in its objectivity, "intuitively grasped", in the terminology either of Jacob or of the Latin epistemological discussion mentioned in pp. 8–10 of Chapter 1 above) correlated with the iconic representation in which the idea psychologically considered exists as but the fundament for the (suprasubjective and at least prospectively intersubjective) relation in which the idea semiotically considered consists and which terminates at the physically objective structure or feature in question.[1] The iconic representation in which the idea psychologically considered consists, in short, is not the idea as sign. The psychological condition or state giving rise to an affective or cognitive relation is merely a *sign-vehicle* or fundament for the suprasubjective relation which constitutes the sign itself by objectifying, at one term, its "content" or "referent" and presenting, at the other term, this content to the organism correlated psychologically here and now (in the *Innenwelt*) with the objective content (of the *Umwelt*).

We saw above that physical relations are distinguished by having no intrinsic nature other than indirectly through the subjective (or, we may now add, objective) terms that they relate. We saw too that relations involved in sensation are not only objective but at the same time physical relations. What the *Tractatus de Signis* is calling our attention to at this point is that even those relations involved in perception which do not bear on anything here and now physically existing as such are no different as relations from those involved in perception

---

[1] See especially the materials on relation added to the electronic edition of *Tractatus de Signis*, Σ21: Article 5. "Whether Relation is Formally Terminated at Something Absolute or at Something Relative" (Reiser 1930: 595b25–600b23).

(such as those of sensation) that do bear on something here and now existing physically as such. For every relation as such refers its subject to that which the subject itself is not, and this is no less true when an apprehensive relation terminates at an object or aspect of an object lacking physical instantiation than when it terminates at an object or aspect thereof existing physically as well as objectively.[2]

Considering then the case when a given relation is and the case when it is not objective, the relation in question is able to be *in either case* physical depending only on the circumstance external to the relation itself of whether the terminus of the relation has a material correlate in the environment formally corresponding with the fundament of the relation. The only difference in the hypothetical two cases is that while objective relations, in order to be physical, must terminate at something physically real, yet when they terminate at what is not physically real, either through a strategy to bring about a state of affairs not yet existent, or through an error of apprehension, or through an error of judgment, they remain nonetheless relations; by contrast, merely physical relations cease to exist as relations when the environmental features at which they terminate (their "termini") cease, though their fundaments continue to exist as the aspects of physical subjectivity which supported the relations while they perdured.

This is why "it suffices to be a sign virtually in order to signify in act", in the famous formula of the *Tractatus de Signis* (Book I, Question 1, 126/3–4), as can be seen most easily through a concrete example.[3]

---

2   I first discussed this point in 1975 ("Reference to the Non-Existent"); after twenty-one years, the discussion has been picked up, though obtusely, in an analytic journal (Haldane 1996). Such is the pace of "progress" in philosophy.

3   The example given in the text of the *Tractatus de Signis* at this point is highly abstract, and the exposition of the example not as clear as might be. One gets the feeling that the author of the text was, at this juncture, experiencing the groping that normally accompanies the breaking of new ground (Book I, Question 1, 126/1–22): "And to the proof: 'It [the footprint of a dead ox, the statue of a dead emperor, etc.] signifies formally, i.e., in act, therefore it is formally a sign,' the

Consider the case of a dinosaur bone, the type of case we will return to at the end of this chapter. As a sign-vehicle, it exists in nature with only a virtual signification. But if discovered and recognized for what it is, by that virtual signification it leads the mind to form an actual signification terminating at an objective awareness of the no longer existent animal to whom the bone actually belonged in the past. The rationale of moving and stimulating the cognitive powers of the paleontologist are in the bone as a physical subjectivity transcendentally relative to the former animal. Upon this foundation, and guided by it as recognized or known, the mind is able to supply in objective being the actual relation to the dinosaur which

consequence is flatly denied, because it suffices to be a sign virtually in order to signify in act. This can be readily seen in an example: X in act causes and produces an effect, therefore it is in act really a cause; for when the cause in question no longer exists in itself, through the virtuality or efficacy it leaves behind, it causes and causes formally, because the effect is then formally produced. Just so, when a sign exists and by a virtual signification formally leads the mind to something signified [which no longer exists in fact], it is nevertheless not a sign formally, but virtually and fundamentally. For since the rationale of moving or stimulating the mind remains, which comes about through the sign insofar as it is something representative, even if the relation of substitution for the signified does not remain, the sign is able to exercise the functions of substituting without the relation, just as a servant or minister can perform the operations of his ministry even when the master, to whom he bespeaks a relation, and in which relation the rationale of servant and minister formally consists, has died". – "Et ad probationem: 'Formaliter, id est actu significat, ergo formaliter est signum,' negatur liquide consequentia, quia sufficit virtualiter esse signum, ut actu significet. Et instatur manifeste in hac: B actu causat et producit effectum, ergo actu in re est causa; nam ipsa causa non existens in se, per virtutem a se relictam causat et formaliter causat, quia effectus tunc formaliter producitur. Sic existente signo et significatione virtuali formaliter ducit potentiam ad signatum, et tamen formaliter non est signum, sed virtualiter et fundamentaliter. Cum enim maneat ratio movendi potentiam, quod fit per signum, in quantum repraesentativum est, etiamsi non maneat relatio substitutionis ad signatum, potest exercere functiones substituentis sine relatione, sicut servus vel minister potest exercere operationes sui ministerii etiam mortuo domino, ad quem dicit relationem, et in qua formaliter consistit ratio servi et ministri".

formerly existed in physical being. The objective relation here and now and the physical relation which once was are equivalent as relations, differing only in that what formerly provenated from physical being alone now provenates from objective being alone.

The key to reading the *Tractatus de Signis* text on this point is to keep clearly in mind the distinction between sign as *sign-vehicle* and sign *formally as sign* which, in every case, consists in a relation over and above its fundament, and the indifference of relation as suprasubjective to having its source in physical being alone, physical and objective being simultaneously, or objective being alone. For finite minds, the possibility of truth presupposes the possibility of error, and conversely; for both are consequences of the indifference of relation to its subjective ground, the consistence of the being of sign in relation, and the dependency of the finite mind on signs in all that it knows. The *Tractatus de Signis* makes the key distinction nicely:

> in the rationale of something conductive or leading, there are two elements to be considered, to wit, the capacity or rationale of exercising the very representation of the thing to be conveyed, and the relation of subjection to or substitution for that on whose behalf it exercises the representation, just as in the case of a master, both a power of governing or coercing subjects and a relation to them are considered, and in the case of a servant, both a power of obeying and a relation of subjection. As regards the capacity to lead representatively, we grant that it is not a relation according to the way relation has being, but the fundament of [such] a relation; specifically, it is that proportion and connection with the thing signified; but as regards the formality of sign, which is not any proportion and representation, but one subserving and substituted for what is signified, it consists formally in the relation of a substituted representative, just as being a servant or being a master are formally relations, and

yet the right of coercing and of obeying are not relations according to the way they have being.[4]

On this point the unity of semiotic inquiry may be said to hinge: "the fundament of a sign [the sign-vehicle, as we now say] does not formally constitute the rationale of the sign as regards that which formally belongs to subjection and substitution [of sign for signified through a relation according to the way relation has its proper being as transsubjective], but as regards that which belongs to the capacity for arousing or moving";[5] for this is the point that applies equally to the case of so-called natural signs and to the most extreme case of social sign, the stipulated sign:

> Whence just as a natural sign exercises signification by reason of its fundament, even when it does not have a relation in act to what is signified owing to the nonexistence of that particular significate – for example, the statue of the emperor when the emperor himself is dead; so a linguistic sound or mark, even when the relation is not conceived in act and consequently does not exist by means of a concept, still signifies and represents by reason of the imposition once made. This

[4] *Tractatus de Signis*, Book I, Question 1, 126/23–127/6: "in ratione ductivi est duo considerare, scilicet vim seu rationem exercendi ipsam repraesentationem ducendi, et relationem subiectionis seu substitutionis id, pro quo eam exercet, sicut in domino et consideratur potestas gubernandi seu coercendi subditos et relatio ad illos, et in servo potestas obediendi et relatio subiectionis. Quantum ad vim ducendi repraesentative, fatemur non esse relationem secundum esse, sed fundamentum relationis, scilicet illa proportio et connexio cum signato; sed quantum ad formalitatem signi, quae non est quaelibet proportio et repraesentatio, sed subserviens et substituta signato, consistit formaliter in relatione substituti repraesentativi, sicut esse servum vel esse dominum formaliter relationes sunt, et tamen ius coercendi et obediendi relationes secundum esse non sunt".

[5] *Tractatus de Signis*, Book I, Question 1, 128/30–34: "fundamentum signi non constituit formaliter rationem signi, quantum ad id, quod formaliter est subiectionis et substitutionis, sed quantum ad id, quod est virtutis movendi".

imposition does not create the sign formally, but fundamentally and proximately.[6]

Relation, in short, makes the sign in general possible precisely because it is the only aspect of being which does not achieve its proper status in subjectivity, but in transcending subjectivity and connecting one subject with something that that subject itself is not, be that other such merely physically, objectively as well as physically, or only cognitively and purely objectively. Whence signs not only connect the two orders of the physical and the objective, but pass back and forth between the two, sometimes existing only in the one, sometimes only in the other, and sometimes in both (the ideal case of science).

In this light, it is perhaps already too much to say that the proper nature of relation is *intersubjectivity*, for this obtains outside cognition only in the case of physical relations, i.e., relations between subjects here and now existing on both sides of the relational field. What reveals the true essence of the purely relative, after all, is not that it be intersubjective but that it be *transsubjective* or *suprasubjective*, that is, always conveying the individual subject beyond itself and connecting it with some object other than itself, indifferently to the physically subjective dimensions and status of that object. *Renvoi*, for the reasons given elsewhere at length,[7] is the preferred name for the semiosic relation prescissed and thematized within semiotics as the irreducibly triadic relation in which alone the sign possesses and exercises its proper being.

The action of signs is thus revealed as possible in the first place because relations are not tied to a subjective ground

---

6 *Tractatus de Signis*, Book I, Question 1, 130/17–27: "Unde sicut signum naturale ratione sui fundamenti exercet significationem, etiamsi non habeat relationem actu ad signatum, quia tale signatum non existit, ut imago imperatoris ipso mortuo; ita vox vel scriptura, etiamsi actu non concipiatur relatio et consequenter non existat mediante conceptu, adhuc significat et repraesentat ratione impositionis semel factae, quae non reddit formaliter signum, sed fundamentaliter proxime".

7 Jakobson 1974; Deely 1994a: 201–44.

which is necessarily physical. Relations, considered according to this proper being as suprasubjective, may just as well terminate in a pure object or have their foundation in a pure object which has no status here and now other than that of being cognized or known.

But the condition is transitive. A relation which one time is founded on or terminates at an object which is also physically real may at another time be founded on or terminate at an object no longer physically real, and a relation which is founded on or terminates at a physically nonexistent object may at another time be founded on or terminate at an object become physically real. The notion of reality needs to accommodate this actual situation of human experience.

Perhaps no single word is more closely associated with the developments of philosophy and science than the term "reality". Of course, along with any claim to knowing what reality is goes a tacit understanding of what reality means, for "'reality' is also a word, a word which we must learn to use correctly".[8] Probably there is no word of established usage which has been successfully constrained to a single sense, and this term "reality" is no exception. Even so, it seems to be one of the terms most closely associated with the awakening of human understanding to a realization of its difference from the perception of sense, inasmuch as it seems most centrally to convey a sense of there being a prejacent given respecting the desires and wishes of any human individual, or indeed of any human community. The corruption that almost at once invades this sense is the suspicion that *only* what is independent in this prejacent manner belongs to "nature", the real, or is "really real". Fine as far as it goes, this notion of reality in terms of the prejacent structures of the physical world, in particular, forms the principal heritage of this term as we pass from the Greeks to the Latins, and no less so as we pass from Latin times to modernity.

For as scientific understanding began to displace philosophy from the central role in the academies and culture of

---

[8] The excellent formulation of this point is attributed to Neils Bohr, in French and Kennedy 1985: 302.

Western civilization after the seventeeth century, one thing that did not change, at least at first, was an uncompromising sense of 'reality' as a natural world prejacent to and independent of the human mind, a world governed in its interactions by laws which form the proper object of human understanding, laws and interactions which formed the object and goal of understanding of the natural philosophers from the remotest times in their pursuit of a science called by the Stoics and Aristotelians alike "physics", *scientia, seu philosophia, naturalis.*

What changed in the seventeeth century was not at all this notion of reality as the mind-independently real or 'given', but only the methodological convictions about how this world of nature could best be penetrated by human understanding. In the ancient physics, the emphasis had been upon an intelligible content superior to what the senses could attain even in the most refined achievements of perception, imagination, and estimation of material possibilities, a content to which the general designation of "being" (ov, *ens*) was assigned, which found its most refined assessment in "first philosophy", which eventually came to be called "metaphysics" and, much later, "ontology".[9] The modern physics changed not the goal of knowing the prejacent reality, but only the emphasis on being as distinct from the observable, and the methods of dialectic and logic as the way to bring out for the understanding the proper content of the real. In place of dialectic, the moderns urged observation, and in place of deduction (*syllogismus*) they recommended mathematical inference which would enable precise calculations of consequences and expectations in the realm of what can be observed. The final goal of the inquiry, however, for the early moderns at least, remained unquestioned and unchanged. It was not by accident that Newton labeled his watershed work (1686–1687) *Principia Mathematica Philosophiae Naturalis.* To all intents and purposes, the expression "natural philosophy" has fallen out of use today; but it was the favored Latin

[9]   See Deely 1967 and 1987.

expression for the science of φύσις the science of nature or *physics*, of Aristotle, and was common to almost the end of modern times.[10]

Many and interesting controversies attended the change from the ancient to the modern approach to developing the science of physics. Perhaps the most important issues were less of a methodological character than a question of proper standpoint, for the moderns aimed to establish that the controlling principles in a science mathematical in form and experimental in its matter are of a radically different character from whatever knowledge of nature may be possible in the guise of intelligible being unfolded by the understanding according to the form of logical principles resident in the structure of natural language.[11] But the most useful and important of these controversies were, in effect, undermined from the beginning of modernity by a still more fundamental shift within philosophy itself from physical being to the discourse within and through which whatever is known of being is developed and communicated. This shift, not as any matter of principle, but simply as a matter of the way in which it was in fact accomplished, slowly corroded the very notion and sense itself of prejacent physical reality as the consequences of the epistemological principle that had been accepted, effectively, without question – namely, that the mind itself in and through its cognitive activity forges its direct object of experience at every level – more and more plainly demonstrated an incompatibility with the pretension to achieve *any* knowledge of physical being, *any* apprehension of any reality beyond that of the mind's own workings.

This result was neither the expectation nor the intent of the early moderns, who had set themselves enthusiastically to

---

[10] It can still be found in the 19th century catalogues of college and university courses. See the gloss on the References on Newton's *Principia*, p. 140 ff, below.

[11] Perhaps the best late modern summary of these issues in English form is to be found in Maritain 1941 and 1959 (the former may be regarded as an extremely brief abstract or précis of the latter, which first appeared in French in 1932 and underwent many editions).

reinforce the change from ancient to modern physics; it proved to be merely the principal result among those several "remarkable propositions" of modern philosophy which "capture the understanding so to speak against its own will", in Kant's able description from 1747 cited earlier.[12] In shifting their own focus from being to discourse, from ontology to epistemology, the early moderns initially saw themselves as endorsing the dissatisfaction with over-reliance on textual sources logically exposed in detailed commentaries (as had become the established procedure of the scholastics[13]) and

[12] In Chapter 1, p. 7, above.

[13] Although sometimes I wonder to what extent this objection of the times, apparently directed against the Aristotelian philosophers, a safe target, is not the more intended for the unsafe target of the theologians, who in fact have always been the far more culpable in this area from the earliest Christian times. I think of such examples as that of Cosmas Indicopleustes with his *Christian Topography* (Alexandria, i.535–47), "in which he refutes the impious opinion that the earth is a globe", for "the Christian geography was forcibly extracted from the texts of scripture, and the study of nature was the surest symptom of an unbelieving mind. The orthodox faith confined the habitable world to one temperate zone, and represented the earth as an oblong surface, four hundred days' journey in length, two hundred in breadth, encompassed by the ocean, and covered by the solid crystal of the firmament"(Gibbon 1788: 250, text and note 78). But examples of equal or greater offensiveness can easily be culled from every tradition of sacred, "revealed" texts, both before and outside of the Christian development. Surely, within the Christian era, one of the more outstanding examples of hermeneutic abuse is the career of the "blessed" Robert Cardinal Bellarmine (1542–1621) who, well in advance of the most famous trials over which he held sway (in 1600 that of Bruno, in 1616 that of Copernicus' work, laying the ground for the 1633 condemnation of Galileo), had arrived through scriptural study at a detailed cosmology which he regarded as "virtually revealed". These astonishing results he recorded between 1570 and 1572 in his unpublished Commentary on Qq. 65–74 of Aquinas c.1266, autographs which we may hope will one day be brought to full publication (Baldini and Coyne 1984 is barely a start) to add to the many object-lessons still resisted that make up the unending "Galileo Affair": see Blackwell 1991: esp. 40–45, 104–6 (on the truth of the Bible even in trivial matters being guaranteed as Bellarmine put it, *ex parte dicentis* – "because of God being the one who says so"). Too

promoting the search for new methods which would place the science of physics on a new footing actually based on nature rather than on the interpretations of nature conveyed in authoritative texts. The celebrated Discours de la méthode of 1637, by which Descartes prefaced his investigations into substantive natural philosophy, has survived as an independent essay long after his substantive investigations have proven hopelessly archaic from the point of view of science.

Every new beginning has its perils. In the case of the early modern initiators of what came to be the classical modern mainstream of philosophical inquiry (eventually clearly distinct from modern scientific inquiry), what proved fatal was their unexamined assumption that the ideas of the human mind are themselves the direct objects of human experience.[14]

bad Galileo, writing in 1615 with Bellarmine in mind as well as still alive (see Blackwell 1991: 274), felt constrained to leave unpublished his observation that "those who try to refute and falsify [propositions about the physical world] by using the authority of . . . passages of Scripture will commit the fallacy called 'begging the question'. For since the true sense of the Scripture will already have been put in doubt by the force of the argument, one cannot take it as clear and secure for the purpose of refuting the same proposition. Rather one needs to take the demonstrations apart and find their fallacies with the aid of other arguments, experiences, and more certain observations. And when the truth of fact and of nature has been found in this way, then, but not before, can we confirm the true sense of Scripture and securely use it for our purposes. Thus again the secure path is to begin with demonstrations, confirming the true and refuting the false". This lesson applies across the cultures to every group that draws upon texts deemed revealed, not in every case, indeed, but wherever arise questions that can be investigated and resolved by means of natural investigations, scientific or philosophical.

[14] In Kant, it is true, the radical subjectivism of Descartes and Locke will be replaced by a relational theory of representations, but the central point is yet maintained: that, in the relation to objects, the ideas (or "representations") of the knower alone provide constitutively the direct objects of all experience, beginning with sensation itself, and so veil behind their objective termini whatever there be of the order the Latins styled *ens reale*. That is why the attempt most recently illustrated in Collins (1999) to conclude that Kant is indeed a realist, since for him outer reality is independent of us, is not only rarely but always futilely made: it misses the point.

Differences soon developed among the moderns over the relative emphasis to be given to rational and mathematical analysis versus experiment and observation in the understanding of nature, giving rise to the quarrels of "empiricists" with "rationalists". But these differences served only to distract from and gloss over the common assumption which united all the moderns, an assumption which sank ever deeper into the background and foundation of the various edifices of modern philosophical thought which were subsequently raised.

The curious result of the celebrated rationalist-empiricist controversy was that, without exception, the modern philosophers in both camps found themselves completely baffled to explain how the realist pretensions and hopes of the new physics, or any physics, could be warranted in terms of epistemological theory, the theory of knowledge. The problem was not in starting with knowledge or mind, as neoscholastics of the late nineteenth and twentieth century were to urge. The problem was a radically semiotic one, the failure to distinguish between representations and objects at the level of ideas, and, at this same level, between signs and *sign-vehicles*, a failure rendered all the more fatal and irremediable by the poverty of modern analyses of the notion of relation in its indifference to the physical, the psychological, and the objective alike. With hardly a second thought or even first consideration, the classical authors of mainstream modernity were content to assign all relations as such, all "pure" relations, to the comparative work of mind elaborating cognition.[15]

---

[15] Given the notorious quarrelsomeness of philosophers and their reputation of never agreeing on anything, it is amusing to find that the mainstream modern authors all concur in denying of relation any participation in the fact or even notion of prejacent reality. See the late modern classic of Weinberg 1965. This view is directly relevant to the idea of substance that came to prevail in modernity, as we saw illustrated in the text of Kant cited in the discussion earlier. We noted above that the Latins themselves bore some responsibility for the unpragmaticistic use of "transcendental" that Kant settled upon, and this can be further illustrated by the description the *Tractatus de Signis* gives of one of the Latin versions of the theory of relation that came

So rose with Berkeley the first explicitation of idealism in the distinctively modern sense of that term, and with Hume skepticism also in the modern sense. Kant, the master of all the moderns in philosophy and the systematizer of an idealism so ruthless as to strangle even the hope of a knowledge of whatever of nature be in any sense prejacent to and independent of human thinking,[16] nonetheless took it for a scandal "to philosophy and to human reason in general" that no proof of the existence of a mind-independent natural world had so far been given.[17] Modern idealism arose in philosophy not so

to be the core modern doctrine (1632: 80/13–81/5: "Speaking therefore of relations in the sense that applies according to the way they have being as distinguished from every subjective or 'absolute' entity . . . some think that relations do not belong to things except according to objective being, and are only intentional affections or conditions by which we compare one thing to another. Whence they constitute relations [i.e., make them consist] not in a respect, but in a comparison; in the order of physical being, to the extent that this exists in contrast to objective being, however, [they hold that] all relations are according to the way being must be expressed in discourse, because a related thing is nothing but an independent or absolute thing known through a comparison to another". – "Loquendo ergo de relationibus in hac sententia prout distinguuntur ab omni entitate absoluta quod solum convenit relationibus secundum esse, aliqui . . . existimant relationes non convenire rebus nisi secundum esse obiectivum et solum esse intentionales affectiones, quibus rem unam alteri comparamus. Unde non in respectu, sed in comparatione relationes constituunt; in re autem omnes relationes esse secundum dici, quia nihil aliud est relatum quam res absoluta cognita per comparationem ad aliud".

How this modern view impacts on any attempt to establish a general rationale of the sign can best be seen through the early modern work of Suárez: see note 2, pp. 44–45 in Poinsot 1632; and compare the whole First Preamble thereto, "De Ente Rationis", with the recent translation by Doyle (1995) of Suárez 1597: Disp. 54 "De Entibus Rationis".

16 *Pace* his self-image as not belonging to the camp of idealism, a view to which only he and the smallest of remnants proved sufficiently deluded to subscribe (see note 14 in this chapter, p. 58 above).

17 Kant 1787: 34n*a*. More remarkable, in line with the observation in the preceding note, he alone fancied that in fact, with the second edition of his *Critique of Pure Reason*, he had successfully provided the wanted

much by intent as by default, Mr. Hyde to the healthy Dr. Jekyll of modern science, as it were (to create an allegory for the modern situation from a fictional story of the period[18]). To the contemporary reader, who presupposes the possibility and fact of communication almost as unconsciously as the early moderns presupposed the identity of ideas with the direct objects of experience, such a situation seems almost incredible.

What is of interest to us here, however, is not the details of the modern epistemological conundrums with the ancient, medieval, and modern idea of a prejacent physical world as the paradigm referent of the term "reality".[19] What is of interest to us rather is the simple fact that by itself this previous notion will no longer do. Even in order to accord the notion its proper validity as far as it goes we need to recognize how and why this notion is derivative rather than primary, arrived at from within rather than prior to our elaboration of and socialization into an objective world. It is an idea which needs not to be rejected, as finally happened in modernity as the consequences of the irremediably nonsemiotic epistemological paradigm that defined its philosophical epoch were explicitly

proof. In my view, the scandal to philosophy was not that such a proof had not been given, but that a view of human knowledge and experience had come to prevail in modernity which made the idea of such a proof wanting in the first place. The further idea of Kant that he had successfully given such a "proof" betrays a very strange notion of demonstration, and is itself a scandal for philosophy, albeit a rather weak, second-order scandal. For the details of this threefold scandal, see Deely 1992: esp. n. 9.

18   To wit, Stevenson 1886. Detailed application of the allegory is made in Deely 2001: Ch. 13.

19   To all this, indeed, semiotic provides a welcome and long-overdue alternative, an idea whose time has come, thankfully revolutionary respecting the past of philosophy and science alike. What is new with semiotics is the frame of reference, the perspective, in which the sign is seen to mediate knowledge over time (*eo ipso* historically) regardless of the logical methods characteristically employed by a given discipline, be it humanistic or scientific; and the realization that semiosis, the action of signs, is a correspective and cumulative process, a process structured by and structuring of "reality". See "The Semiotic Definition of Reality" (Deely 1986a: Section 3); and cf. Ransdell 1986.

worked out. It is an idea which needs only to be subalternated to experience as *one* of the basic directions in which research can be conducted from within the objective world, the other basic direction being the investigation of the proper creations of mind – the spheres of society and culture.

And there needs to be disseminated the further understanding that these are not two separately encapsulated spheres, as Vico whispered fairly early (1725) in the modern ear, but rather mutually compenetrating dimensions of the one sphere of human experience, the objective world which both transcends and partially incorporates within its directly given objectivities something of the famously prejacent physical environment, both in its "natural" being and in those today far more common incarnations of human intelligence in the form of the "artificial" being of the material constructions of human civilization that we encounter as streets and roads, monuments and buildings, territorial and property boundaries, etc.

Even the physical world is not wholly a question of nature, because our access to it is only as part of the objective world wherein *both* aspects of the physical environment through which we encounter nature *and* aspects of culture (often embedded in physical structures hardly natural) are on a par, directly experienced and objectified in their proper being as a purchase for survival and inquiry. The semiosis of sensation provides just that purchase – but in classical modern philosophy, not only that semiosis was precluded (excluded, of course, in theory; it could not be excluded *in actu exercito*), but as well the semiosis proper to the actively interpretive levels of perception and understanding. The moderns located what was proper to perception at the level of sensation; but, even at the level of understanding itself, apart from the empiricist tendency to reduce it to perception, the moderns had no way to handle it as *semiosis*. For they had no room for the sign as a pure relation in its difference from the various sign-vehicles, and no room for the objective order in its difference both from the psychological subjectivity of ideas and from the physical subjectivity of environmental things.

We need, in short, at the outset of the postmodern era, a specifically semiotic notion of reality. For what is distinctive about the action of signs, in contrast to the physical interactions of material objects and things within the environment, may be put at this juncture quite clearly: physical interactions can only take place between things (or also between objects insofar as they have a physical dimension, i.e., insofar as they are at the same time things), whereas the action of signs is indifferent to the physical status of the object signified. And this indifference in turn is possible because the triadic sign-relation participates as a relation in the being peculiar to all relations whereby every relation as such transcends the subjectivity of individual beings, or "substances", with all the individual characteristics or traits ("accidents") that distinguish them as subjects of action and interaction or units of objectification, collective or individual.

It is not, however, as physical that relations achieve this indifference to the physical status of their object. Indeed, precisely as physical, a relation is not indifferent to the physical status of its termination: if the terminus does not physically exist, neither does the physical relation. Only in semiosis is the possible indifference of relation to the physical status of its term realized, and this is why the sign relation cannot be identified with any physical relation as such, even though a physical relation, as such dyadic, may well be made *also* part of – an arm within – a sign relation as such triadic.[20]

Three basic cases can be distinguished. There is the case, first, of a physical relation existing now apart from and now as incorporated within a semeiosy. There is the case, second,

---

[20] From *Tractatus de Signis*, Book I, Question 2, 137 note 4 (editorially appended from the 1663 Lyons text): "Similarly, those relations by which a sign can be proportioned to a signified are formally other than the sign-relation itself, e.g., the relation of effect to cause, of similitude or image, etc., even though some recent authors confound the sign-relation with these relations, but unwarrantably: because to signify or to be caused or to be similar are diverse exercises in a sign. For in signifying, a substitution for the principal significate is exercised, that that principal may be manifested to a power, but in the

of an objective relation which, because its terminus exists in the environment, is also a physical relation. And there is the case, third, of an objective relation which, as part of a semeiosy, is objective even though its significate term has no physical existence, whether never, merely not yet, or simply no longer. But what distinguishes the third case from the first two reveals in particular what distinguishes physical interaction from semiosis: physical interactions can transpire only when both terms of the interaction exist, but the action of signs always involves three terms of which the term signified need not exist in order for the action to transpire.[21]

Brute interactions, as Peirce would eventually put it, are inherently dyadic, while semiosis is always triadic. In principle (however multiple the things actually involved in a given physical occurrence), brute secondness always relates two

rationale of a cause or an effect is included nothing of an order to a cognitive power; wherefore they are distinct fundaments, and so postulate distinct relations. These relations, moreover, can be separated from the sign-relation, just as a son is similar to the father and his effect and image, but not a sign. The sign-relation therefore adds to these relations, which it supposes or prerequires in order to be habilitated and proportioned to this significate rather than to that one". – "Similiter relationes illae, quibus signum proportionare potest ad significatum, diversae sunt formaliter a relatione ipsa signi, e.g. relatio effectus vel causae, similitudinis vel imaginis etc., licet aliqui recentes confundant relationem signi cum istis relationibus, sed immerito: tum quia diversum exercitium est in signo significare vel causari aut similem esse. In significando enim exercetur substitutio principalis signati, ut manifestetur potentiae, in ratione vero causae aut effectus nihil de ordine ad potentiam includitur; quare distincta fundamenta sunt, et sic distinctas relationes postulant. Et praeterea separari possunt relationes istae a relatione signi, sicut filius est similis patri et effectus eius et imago, non tamen signum. Addit ergo relatio signi super illas relationes, quas supponit aut praerequirit, ut habilitetur et proportionetur huic signato potius quam illi". See further Book I, Question 3, 160/10–21, and the discussion in note 13 of that same Question, pp. 163–64. For the bearing of these texts on the notion of interpretant, see Ch. 6, note 31, p. 105 below.

[21] For more detailed discussion of this point, see Deely 1990: 23ff., 1994 throughout, and "Mediation of the objective" in 1994a: 223–26. Cf. also the discussion in Colapietro 1994.

things, but semiosis mediates between physical and objective being by referring one thing to another in terms of a common third. And what is referred to may be merely an object without physical status, for whatever reason (having passed out of physical existence, having never existed physically in the first place, or mayhap being impossible of physical existence in any case – as in the world of so-called ideal objects of utopian, mathematical, and logical types, which can only be accessed on this planet through species-specifically human language).

But even in the purely physical order relations as such exhibit an anticipation of the indirectness of semiosis' thirdness:[22]

> And though a cause is required for every entity and form, yet in a special sense a fundament is said to be required for a relation, because other forms require a cause only in order to be produced in being and exist, whereas relation – owing to its minimal entitative character and because in terms of its proper concept it is toward another – requires a fundament not only in order to exist but also in order to be able to remain in existence, that is, in order to be a mind-independent rationale of physical being.

Moreover, since physical relations can remain in their fundaments (as "transcendental relatives") even when the condition for their physical being as relations – that they have physical termini as such – no longer prevails, we can readily see why objective natural signs "function differently", as the *Tractatus de Signis* puts it,[23] in the way they pressure the mind

---

[22] *Tractatus de Signis*, Second Preamble, Article 2, 88/17–28: "Et licet ad omnem entitatem et formam requiratur causa, specialiter tamen ad relationem dicitur requiri fundamentum, quia aliae formae solum requirunt causam, ut producantur in esse et existant, relatio autem propter suam minimam entitatem et quia ex proprio conceptu est ad aliud, requirit fundamentum non solum ut existat, sed etiam ut sit capax existendi, id est ut sit entitas realis".

[23] See the text cited in Ch. 6, note 26, p. 98 below.

in the direction of an understanding of their significates as compared with objective conventional signs. Since the potential sign-vehicle in the case of an objective natural sign is a physical structure which would motivate or privilege some lines of interpretation over others, prospective signs of this type have a capacity to force or lead the mind in the course of their being progressively objectified that is rooted in the physical being itself of what is objectified as able to found and warrant objective relations according to the very pattern in which it once necessitated physical ones (recall the expression from the *Tractatus* characterizing such relatives: "rei absolutae imbibita"[24]). The "nonarbitrary" or "motivated" character of the connection between the sign-relation and its physical vehicle in such a case provides a circumstance[25] which sharply differentiates such signs from the situation and condition of linguistic signs, whose vehicle is only culturally correlated with its significate by a convention or code in the stead of any physical "motivation" as such (the famous "arbitrariness" of linguistic sign-vehicles outside the context of the habit structure of a community).

Using the term "thought" for what I would call objective being in the sense of "knowable as such" (through the addition of the requisite relation to a cognitive organism), regardless of what is actually known, and "sign" for the *sign-vehicle* of a transcendental relative in the Latin sense, Max Fisch has described the manner in which signs, as consisting in pure relations according to a being deriving indifferently from thought or from physical nature, draw the physical order

---

[24] *Tractatus de Signis*, 90/24–26: "a transcendental relation is not a form adventitious to a subject or absolute thing, but one assimilated to it, yet connoting something extrinsic upon which the subject depends or with which it is engaged" – "relatio transcendentalis non est forma adveniens subiecto seu rei absolutae, sed illi imbibita, connotans tamen aliquid extrinsecum, a quo pendet vel circa quod versatur".

[25] *Ibid.*: 90/33–34: "a transcendental relation is in the absolute entity itself and does not differ from its [subjective] being" – "transcendentalis sit in ipsa entitate absoluta nec ab eius esse differat".

itself into the objective world of human understanding, the Lebenswelt[26] in its difference from Umwelt:[27]

> Marine fossils found on a mountain are interpreted by the paleontologist as signs of the sea level having been higher than the level of deposit of those fossils, at far distant dates the paleontologist proceeds to estimate. But the number of such fossils that ever has been, and perhaps that ever will be, accessible to paleontologists or to other interpreters is an extremely small fraction of their total number. Those that never have been and that never will be interpreted are nonetheless signs. Again, how extremely rare is it for an ill human being or other animal to be observed at all by a trained and skilled diagnostician, and how much escapes even the most skilled! But the symptoms and other signs are there, and so are the interpretants to which they *would* lead an equally qualified observer and interpreter. The thought is "there", though there be no thinker of it.

Thus the distinctiveness of semiosis is verified, equally in fact, when all three of the terms joined by semeiosy have a physical existence and when only two of them, indeed, when only *one* of them (the "psychological" term or "pole") so exist. The case of the nonexistent object signified is only the sharp exacerbation to the point of disclosure of what is true of all semiosis as such.

---

[26] This term, which is but a proposed alternative for the term "Umwelt" when the Umwelt in question is a species-specifically human one, will occur several times in our text. For a specific discussion of its rationale, the reader may look ahead to p. 112 in Chapter 7 below.

[27] Fisch 1979: 360.

Chapter 6

A Semiosis beyond Perception

So far we have spoken of semiosis in sensation and perception. There is also semiosis in nature and in human understanding as distinct from both perception and sensation. Semiosis in nature goes beyond our present purview;[1] but the semiosis peculiar to human understanding is at the heart of the matter before us. Since human understanding finds its operational existence initially in terms of the intersemiosis which perception makes possible as developing around a sensory core, to speak of understanding without first establishing the perceptual frame-work upon which understanding depends for its materials, and within which it makes its own further arrangements, would be difficult or impossible. But we are in a position at this point to see how understanding,

---

[1] See Krampen 1981 for the original extension of semiosis to the plant world in a programmatic statement, commented upon in Deely 1982a; for extension beyond this to physical nature in its full extent see: "The Doctrine of Signs" (Sebeok 1986); "The Grand Vision" (Deely 1989, but correctly reprinted in Deely 1994a: 183–200); and "Physiosemiosis and Phytosemiosis" (Deely 1990: Chapter 6); "How is the universe perfused with signs?" (Deely 1997a); "Physiosemiosis and Semiotics" (Deely 1998); and "The Reach of Textuality" (Deely 1999).

arising within perception, goes beyond it.[2] Understanding restructures the objective world of animal perception principally by introducing into it new objective patterns (new relationships) which make accessible to human thought structures and beings which, as objective, are entirely hidden to all other biological species on this planet.

Examples of beings introduced into objectivity through the medium of species-specifically human language, with lit-

---

[2] "It is not necessary that everything known in the understanding or cognized by internal sense should be apprehended by the external senses. It is enough if all those things are virtually contained in the formal specification that is emitted by the sensible object and then by sense, and can be unfolded in the higher power. Thus St. Thomas says in the *Summa Theologica*, I, q. 78, art. 4, reply to objection 4, that 'although the operation of the understanding arises out of sense, the understanding yet cognizes many facets of the thing apprehended through sense that sense cannot perceive, and the same holds for the estimative power, although to a lesser extent.' It can well be, therefore, that something can be known through internal sense that is not known directly and formally by external sense, but that is some modality or respect founded on those sensibles and virtually contained in them." – "Et non est necesse, quod omnia, quae cognoscuntur in intellectu vel sensu interno, sint cognita per sensum externum, sed sufficit, quod in specie, quae emittitur ab obiecto et deinde a sensu, virtualiter contineantur illa omnia et explicari possint in potentia superiori. Et sic dicit D. Thomas 1. p. q. 78. art. 4. ad 4., 'quod licet operatio intellectus oriatur a sensu, tamen in re apprehensa per sensum intellectus multa cognoscit, quae sensus percipere non potest, et similiter æstimativa, licet inferiori modo.' Itaque bene potest cognosci per sensum internum aliquid, quod directe et formaliter a sensu externo non cognoscatur, sed sit modus aliquis seu respectus fundatus in illis sensibilibus et in eis virtualiter contentus" (from Poinsot 1635: 263b41–64a11, included in the 1985 Deely edition of the *Tractatus de Signis* as note 3 at 67/9; cross-refer the text in Ch. 4, note 3, p. 39 f. above).

Thus, besides the relations perception introduces to form sensations into objects perceived and the relations understanding introduces into the objects of perception, there are also relations understanding generates on the basis of its proper activity as distinct from what is proper to perceptual activity, principal among them being, I would argue, the self-relation of objects which gives rise to intelligibility in the first place: see the discussions later in this chapter, pp. 76–77 and 106–9; and in Ch. 9, pp. 113–14, esp. 114 f., note 5.

tle or no regard for actual existence in historically verifiable clues of physical existence and embodiment, abound in human history. They provide, for example, the legendary ancestry actually claimed for various peoples, much of the population of medieval bestiaries, and various national or regional heroes who, like the Cid of Spain, owe virtually all that they are objectively to the credulity and aspirations of some region. It may be enough to cite one of the more captivating examples likely to be nominally familiar to every reader:[3]

> . . . enriched with the various, though incoherent, ornaments which were familiar to the experience, the learning, or the fancy of the twelfth century . . . every nation embraced and adorned the popular romance of Arthur and the Knights of the Round Table; their names were celebrated in Greece and Italy; and the voluminous tales of Sir Lancelot and Sir Tristram were devoutly studied by the princes and nobles, who disregarded the genuine heroes and historians of antiquity. At length the light of science and reason was rekindled; the talisman was broken; the visionary fabric melted into air; and, by a natural, though unjust, reverse of the public opinion, the severity of the present age is inclined to question the *existence* of Arthur.

But it is not only myths and legends historically distorted or outright false that are at stake in this peculiar power of human understanding to effect, through its species-specifically unique language, the consideration of objective beings on a par in cognition with the physical existence of rocks and stars in the material universe. The very existence of science itself as an investigative process depends on just this power to conceive what is other than our senses and sense perception directly inform us to be the case about the being or appearance of the surrounding universe. Philosophy, too, equally trades on this peculiar power to create objectivities detached

[3]   Gibbon 1781a: 162–63.

>70<

from any sure linkage with the physical surroundings, past, present, or future.

Just this circumstance arises as a consequence of the fact that mind-dependent and mind-independent relations are objectively undifferentiated in their structure *as* relations: we can be deceived and cannot always tell when a relationship we have posited for the purpose of understanding some structure – be it physical or cultural or some set of relationships which, taken together, constitute in their nexus some object – is real or unreal. We perforce rely on models in order to answer the question what something is, and models are systems of objective relations which may or may not be duplications of a system of *physical* relations as well. This is why Aquinas could say that "even the being of an essence is a kind of being of reason".[4] Insofar as the model is an accurate model, that is, insofar as it actually models the physical structure we seek to understand, it provides us with the essence, the "quiddity", of the structure in question, whether that structure be natural or cultural. But of course, *how far* or *whether at all* a given model is accurate is just the problem. Semiotics, as the study of the action of signs, is also the doctrine of *fallibilism*, the science of the possibility of being mistaken.

These creations of the understanding, often enough, may succeed in objectifying some feature of the physical world which in fact exists even though it has never previously been brought into the ken of sense perception, for example, when a planet is predicted by calculation and subsequently telescopes reveal the postulated entity to coincide with an actual planet. In such a case, the hiddenness of the object is merely de facto, say, a circumstance of spatial location. More interesting are the cases where the understanding forges an objectification that is not accessible to any sense in principle, not simply as a matter of spatial location. Into such a category falls the centuries of debate over the existence of God, and similarly the magnificent discussions of Aquinas about the choirs of angels and the modalities of angelic communication. About these matters not

---

4   Thomas Aquinas c.1254–1256: *In I sent.* dist. 19. q. 5. art. 1. ad 7: "etiam quidditatis esse est quoddam rationis."

even the most skillful student of zoösemiosis can credibly pretend to elicit opinions from chimpanzees, dolphins, apes, or any other terrestrial species of nonhuman animal.[5] Of equal or greater interest, and of direct importance for human history, are the many creatures, events, and personages that, through the power of semiosis to relate things otherwise than as they merely occur in the physical surroundings, have been objectified in ways that have promoted causes or ideologies far more than any questions of historical truth.

Of course, the other animals can quite well access these new objectivities to whatever extent they are given a physical embodiment falling within the range of the proportion for environmental interaction which constitutes the cognitive powers of those animals.[6] Romulus and Remus may be fictions, but their statues can be perceived, and a passing dog would not hesitate to put such a statue to its own canine use. A sphinx may never be encountered outside the imagination and its monument of stone, but many an animal can see the stone representation, however bereft that perceiving animal may forever remain of a grasp of the mystery that stone construction is able to present to human understanding. The rank of a general may be displayed in stars and stripes visible to any animal; but only the linguistic human animal will come to understand that these visible markings signify a general.[7]

---

[5]   Nor is this an insult to the animals, as their human lovers seem often to take it; for there is not here any question of a lack of intelligence on the animals' part, but simply a matter of the genre of intelligence proper to them as creatures restricted to zoösemioisic means of objectification, wherein relation remains unrecognizable as such for its lack of a directly sensible aspect, and hence the communicative modality of syntactic language as based directly on the grasp of relations as such remained in that respect closed to them. Their discourse is limited to what is directly accessible to their external senses.

[6]   For a general schema of this process, see Deely 1982: text pp. 118–20, diagram p. 119.

[7]   *Tractatus de Signis*, First Preamble, Article 3, 67/1–68/31: "We say that the internal senses [i.e., in our terms, perceptions prescissively taken as such] 'formally speaking' do not form mind-dependent beings, that is, they do not form them by discriminating between mind-

The examples of objective beings which have shaped the public events of human history despite having no other existence

dependent being and physical being, and by conceiving that which is not a being after the pattern of physical being. Materially, however, to cognize a mind-dependent being is to attain the very appearance of a being physically real, but not to discriminate between that which is of the mind and that which is of the physical world. For example, the imaginative power can form a gold mountain, and similarly it can construct an animal composed of a she-goat, a lion, and a serpent, which is the Chimera [of Greek mythology]. But in these constructions the imagination itself attains only that which is sensible or representable to sense. Yet internal sense does not attain the fact that objects so known have a condition relative to non-being, and from this relative condition are said to be constructed, fictive, mind-dependent, or mental – which is formally to discriminate between being and non-being.

"The reason seems clear: internal sense cannot refer to anything except under a sensible rationale; but the fact that that which is represented to it as sensible happens to be opposed to physical being, does not pertain to internal sense to judge, because internal sense does not conceive of being under the rationale of being. The fact, however, of anything's being regarded as a constructed or fictive being formally consists in this, that it is known to have nothing of entitative reality in the physical world, and yet is attained or grasped on the pattern of a physical entity; otherwise, no discrimination is made between mind-independent being and constructed or fictive being, but only that is attained on whose pattern a mind-dependent being is formed. When this object is something sensible, there is no reason why it cannot be known by sense. But sense attains only that which is sensible in an object, whereas the condition relative to the non-being in whose place the object is surrogated and whence it fictively has being, does not pertain to sense. For this reason, sense does not differentiate a constructed being, under the formal rationale of being a construct, from a true being.

"But that sense is able to know fictive being materially is manifestly the case. Not, indeed, from the fact that even external sense can, for example, cognize a fictive color or appearance, because this color, even though it is the color [of a given object] only apparently, is nevertheless not a fictive being, but one true and physical, that is to say, it is something resulting from light. But that sense grasps mind-dependent beings is proved by this fact, that internal sense synthesizes many things which outside itself in no way are or can be. Sense therefore knows something which is in itself a constructed or fictive being, although the fiction itself sense does not apprehend, but only

than that objective one together with their subsequent historical effects translated through human credibilities into shaping influences of human fortune – sometimes, indeed, costing
lives or reputations – are no doubt the most interesting examples of beings known only to the members of our species on
this planet. But the very origin of language itself in the
species-specifically human sense has its roots in this divide
that understanding opens between perception in its original
sensory context and perception as subsequently derivative

that which, in the fictive being, offers itself as sensible." – "Dicimus
'formaliter loquendo' non formare illa, id est discernendo inter ens
rationis et ens reale, et concipiendo id, quod non est ens, ad instar
entis realis. Materialiter autem cognoscere ens rationis est ipsam
apparentiam realis entis attingere, sed non discernere inter id, quod
rationis et realitatis est. V. g. imaginativa potest formare montem
aureum et similiter animal compositum ex capra, leone et serpente,
quod est chimaera. Sed in istis solum attingit id, quod sensibile seu
quoad sensum repraesentabile est. Quod autem habeant habitudinem ad non ens et ex ista habitudine entia ficta seu rationis
dicantur, quod est formaliter discernere inter ens et non ens, sensus
internus non attingit.
  Ratio videtur manifesta, quia sensus internus non potest ferri in
aliquid nisi sub ratione sensibilis; quod autem id, quod sibi reprae-
sentatur ut sensibile, opponatur enti reali, ad ipsum non pertinet
iudicare, quia non concipit ens sub ratione entis.
  Quod autem aliquid accipiatur tamquam ens fictum, formaliter
consistit in hoc, quod cognoscatur nihil entitatis habere in re, et
tamen ad instar entis attingi; alioquin non discernitur inter ens reale
et ens fictum, sed solum attingitur illud, ad cuius instar formatur ens
rationis. Quod quando est aliquid sensibile, non repugnat a sensu
cognosci, sed ad sensum solum pertinet id, quod in illo de sensibili-
tate est attingere, habitudinem vero ad non ens, cuius loco subrogatur
et unde ficte habet esse, ad sensum non pertinet, et ideo ens fictum
sub formali ratione ficti ab ente vero non discernit.Quod vero ens fictum materialiter possit cognoscere sensus, constat manifeste. Non
quidem, quia sensus etiam externus potest v. g. cognoscere colorem
fictum seu apparentem, quia iste color, licet apparenter sit color, non
tamen est ens fictum, sed verum et reale, scilicet aliquid ex luce resul-
tans. Sed ex eo probatur, quia sensus internus multa ad invicem componit, quae extra se nullo modo sunt aut esse possunt. Cognoscit ergo
aliquid, quod in se est ens fictum, licet ipsam fictionem non apprehendat, sed solum id, quod in illo ente ficto tamquam sensibile se
offert".

also from the activity of understanding. Perception derivative (or subsequently molded) in this way adds to its originally sensory context objective structures escaping sense entirely, particularly as expressed in the developed form constituted by the exaptation of species-specifically human language (the human Innenwelt) to communication through the media of speech (so-called "sign language" as well as the spoken exaptation) and writing.[8]

As we noted earlier, every species can be said to have a species-specific apprehension and consequent means of communication. This is in no sense unique to the human species; every species lives in a species-specific objective world, however much that world may be individually varied by actual experiences. But, on this planet, all the diversity of species-specific communicative modalities among animals extant outside the gene pool of *homo sapiens sapiens* reduce to subspecies, or varieties, of perceptual semiosis, which, as we have seen, both reveals and constructs objects according to sensory appearances strictly in terms of the self-interests of the organisms involved. The human animal, by contrast, goes beyond the relation of objects to the self by sometimes asking what are those objects quite apart from any biological interest which we find in them, insofar as they exhibit an independence of relations to us.

It is true that such an inquiry perforce exhibits an "interest" on the part of the organism pursuing it. But the possibility of *such* an interest is consequent upon, rather than consti-

---

[8]   From a semiotic point of view, whether the apprehension rooted in a human Innenwelt is exapted into the publicly accessible Lebenswelt in the form of speech, writing, or gesture is a matter of essential indifference. In terms of a given communication, any one of these can be rendered equivalent. In such a perspective, Saussure's insistence on the priority of speech over writing is a semiotic defect in his work, a kind of blunder. Out of this blunder, semiotically speaking, Derrida fashioned a career.

The term "exaptation", wherever used in the present work, is taken from Gould and Vrba 1982, to signify the application of evolutionary adaptations to new ends beyond that one or ones in terms of which they originally emerged.

tutive of, a unique objectification, under which the inquirer, in order to be able to inquire in this sense – in order, that is, to have the possibility of such an interest – thematizes the experience of a difference between sign-vehicles and other objects which, on the one hand, appear not to reduce entirely to the experience of them, and, on the other hand, ones which patently do so reduce. It is the objective difference which makes possible and gives rise to the subjective interest (when it does arise), a subtle point of reversal crucial to realize. Usually when we speak of the "needs and interests" of an organism we are speaking of something that arises from the physiology of biological heritage. Here we are speaking of an "interest" which, to be sure, presupposes a psychological capacity, but which presupposes more fundamentally a unique objectification in the absence of which the "interest" has no possibility of arising. It is a *vis ab objecto*, not a *vis a tergo* (not a "need" or an "interest" in any remotely Freudian sense, however quickly or to whatever extent such Freudian factors will subsequently become involved), which such questioning expresses. From the side of the subject, the one in whom such an interest is objectively stimulated, then, how is questioning in this mode possible?

The answer of the *Tractatus de Signis* is that inquiry into the subjective being of objects is possible only for a mind – a cognitive organism, let us say – that is able to grasp relations as such in their difference from the terms related, because only such a cognitive capacity is able to grasp the difference within experience, otherwise hidden, between objects (or aspects of objects) which as such wholly reduce to our experience of them and objects which as such give evidence of a hold on existence to which our experience has no choice but to accommodate itself in a more than social way. This is something that animals other than the human – speaking, of course, only for the species on this planet – cannot do.

The reason for this is that, in order to realize such a difference, as we will see below in more detail, the organism must form as such a mind-dependent relation under which the experienced object is seen in a comparison to the being it has in itself. All objects present themselves in a relation to the cognizing organism. From this standpoint, all objective beings are on the same apparent footing. But as soon as the idea is formed of objects which are beings existing in their own right, that is, subjectively *as well as* objectively, by an idea whose object is the relation as such which introduces into some individual objective unity the cognition-dependent (the purely objective) difference between that unity as foundation and that unity as term of a relation of identity, a difference immediately appears within the objective world between relations founded on other relations, which distinguishes the objective world as such (and makes possible species-specifically human language by the way), and relations founded on objects which are also subjects of physical existence which, as physical, appear to exist apart from the relations founded on them, at least insofar as such relations may be purely objective.

There is a difference, therefore, between mind-dependent relations which result from a comparison between sensible appearances as such, always resulting in an objective mind-dependent organization of individuals or aspects of individuality involved in various objective unities, and mind-dependent relations which result from a comparison between pure relational aspects objectified as such obtaining within the objective world or between the objective world as such and the physical environment in its independent (subjective) being.

That all objective relations, whether recognized as relations or not, result from a comparative act of cognition is clear enough. Clear too is the fact that there is a difference between objective comparisons which result in objective relations recognized as such and objective comparisons which result in objective relations recognized not as such but only through their terms, their always in principle foundations and terminations characterizing objective unities in their distinctiveness or "individuality". But what is the basis for this difference in comparative acts on the side of the organism is not, at least in the texts of the *Tractatus de Signis*, as clear as we could wish. It does not seem to be a point which the author of the text addressed head-on. Nonetheless, from what the text does contain, an answer to this question, once posed, can be teased out by implication.

To begin with, the *Tractatus de Signis* text advises somewhat obscurely that a comparative act as giving rise to an objective relation can be either "compositive" or "discursive".[9] A compositive comparison requires the intellectual judgment which separates the invisible to sense pure relation as such in its proper being (*relatio secundum esse*) from its sensible foundation and termination (*relatio secundum diei*). As such, it occurs – and can occur – in anthroposemiosis alone. But a discursive comparison requires only the comparison of

---

[9] First Preamble, Article 3, 69/41–48: "By the phrase 'a comparative act,' however, we understand not only a compositive, in the sense of a judicative, comparison (which pertains to the second operation of the mind), but any cognition whatever that conceives [its object] with a connotation of and an ordering to another – something that can also occur outside of the second operation of the mind, as, for example, when we apprehend a relation through the order to a terminus. A mind-dependent being can come about as the result of a compositive comparison as well as of a discursive comparison." – "Nomine autem 'actus comparativi' non solum intelligimus comparationem compositivam vel iudicativam, quae pertinet ad secundam operationem, sed quamcumque cognitionem, quae cum connotatione et ordine ad aliud concipit, quod etiam extra secundam operationem fieri potest, ut quando apprehendimus relationem per ordinem ad terminum. Potest etiam fieri ens rationis per comparationem compositivam aut discursivam."

Bear in mind, therefore, the traditional scholastic distinction between the *first act* of the mind, which consists simply in awareness, and the *second act* of the mind, which consists in a judgment made on the basis of that of which we are aware. (The *third act* of the mind, namely, reasoning, they saw as consisting in that intellectual process of linking together and developing the consequences of various judgments.) Normally these three "acts" were conceived in purely intellectual terms; but the best authors were well aware that they had each of them perceptual analogies, the development of which, however, and unfortunately, was all but universally neglected among the Latin authors. In this regard, our *Tractatus de Signis* text was highly and fortunately exceptional.

one sensible aspect to another, and hence can occur indifferently in anthroposemiosis or zoösemiosis.[10] That seems clear enough, and, indeed, straightforward. But so described the situation is too simple. For the basis for the prior possibility of the postulated "compositive comparison" is something that must first occur in the discursive comparison, namely, an awareness of relation as such. Whence the *Tractatus de Signis* text further specifies that discursive comparison is prior to and more fundamental than compositive comparison, and that we must distinguish within the discursive comparison itself a twofold basis of discourse, the one which proceeds wholly on the basis of apprehensions of what is directly sensible (which insofar is common to zoösemiosis and anthroposemiosis), and another which proceeds in terms

---

[10] *Tractatus de Signis*, First Preamble, Article 3, 73/16–74/9): Perception or "internal sense so compares or relates one thing to another by forming a proposition and discourse, that the sense does not formally cognize the very ordination of predicate and of subject and of antecedent to consequent by distinguishing a fictive from a physical relation. And similarly, sense cognizes a gold mountain as regards that which is sensible in those represented parts of gold and a mountain, not as regards the rationale of the construction or fiction as distinguished from a mind-independent reality. To cognize in this regard is to cognize not formally that which is constructed in the rationale of a being, but materially that on whose pattern is constructed that which in itself is not. But the extrinsic denomination that follows on the cognition of sense, insofar as an extrinsic denomination is not a mind-dependent relation formally but fundamentally, is then a mind-dependent relation formally when it is cognized on the pattern of a [mind-independent] relation." – "Sensus internus ita comparat unum alteri formando propositionem et discursum, quod ipsam ordinationem praedicati et subiecti, et antecedentis ad consequens formaliter non cognoscit discernendo relationem fictam a reali. Et similiter montem aureum cognoscit quantum ad id, quod sensibile est in illis partibus repraesentatis auri et montis, non quantum ad rationem fictionis, ut distinguitur a realitate. Quod est cognoscere non formaliter id, quod in ratione entis fingitur, sed materialiter id, ad cuius instar fingitur, quod in se non est. Denominatio autem extrinseca, quae sequitur ad cognitionem sensus, in quantum denominatio extrinseca non est formaliter relatio rationis, sed fundamentaliter, tunc autem est formaliter, quando ad instar relationis cognoscitur."

>79<

of comparison of what is not directly sensible, namely, relation as such (*relatio secundum esse*); and this latter discursive comparison, therefore, would, no less than the compositive comparison, be found in anthroposemiosis alone, but would, in addition, be found there as establishing the prior possibility of any compositive comparison.

Moreover, discursive comparisons of this latter variety would seem to be presupposed to and provide the basis for the "compositive" or "judicative" comparison described above, wherein the difference of relation as such from its foundation and termination is not merely apprehended but thematized as such.[11]

These points being made, the *Tractatus de Signis* puts us in a position to characterize the difference, so far as concerns cognition (that is to say, the objective difference), between

---

[11] *Tractatus de Signis*, First Preamble, Article 3, 74/37–48: "The basic awareness of human understanding does not compare one thing to another by affirming or denying, but it does indeed compare by differentiating one thing from another and by attaining the order of one thing to another. . . . Simple apprehension, therefore [i.e., basic intellectual awareness], has enough comparison for forming a mind-dependent being. Moreover, we do not deny to sense perception the formation of a mind-dependent being on the grounds of the absence of comparison [since there are indeed perceptual comparisons as well as intellectual ones], but on the grounds of the absence of a knowing of universality, because sense does not cognize the more universal rationales by discriminating between true being and constructed or fictive being, which is something that simple apprehension does do; for simple [intellectual] apprehension discriminates between categorial things [objects intrinsically bound up with physical dimensions of existence] and those things that are not in a category of mind-independent being [objects which have as such no being beyond objective]." – "Simplex apprehensio non comparat unum alteri affirmando vel negando, bene tamen discernendo unum ab alio et ordinem unius ad alterum attingendo. . . . Habet ergo sufficientem comparationem ad formandum ens rationis. Sensui autem interiori non negamus formationem entis rationis ex defectu comparationis, sed ex defectu universalitatis cognoscendi, quia non cognoscit universaliores rationes discernendo inter ens verum et fictum, quod tamen facit simplex apprehensio; discernit enim praedicamenta ab iis, quae in praedicamento non sunt."

zoösemiosis as such and anthroposemiosis. The apprehension of animals employing signs in purely zoösemiotic terms is exhausted in the experience, manipulation, and control of the sensory aspects of their objective world. What never enters into the objectification proper to sense perception is an awareness that objects experienced depend in their objective structure on a series of relations transparent to sensation but which give to perception at once its connections with the environment and its arrangement of those connections to suit the organism's individual tastes and species-specific needs.[12]

---

[12] From Poinsot 1635: 263b13–41, included in the 1985 Deely edition of *Tractatus de Signis* as note 17 to First Preamble, Article 3, at 73/22: "Relations are not known in perception under the modality proper to relation, that is to say, with a comparison to a term or by discourse, nor are they known in general, but as they obtain on the side of the fundament or as they are exercised therein, not as relation can be apprehended as an actual significate and according to its own being. But the foundation of the relations knowable in perception – that is, internal sense [e.g., 1635: 263a38–39, 265b21: aversion, friendliness, offspring, hostility, parents, etc.] – is the sensible thing itself according as it founds harmony [utility] or disharmony [harmfulness]. But the sensible thing is not sensed in this way by external sense, because that founding of harmony or discord is not color or sound or smell or anything that is perceived by external sense; yet the relation itself as contrasted to [counterdistinguished from] the fundament and as understood comparatively to the terminus is not attained in perceptual evaluation without collation [i.e., the sort of comparison that is possible only consequent on the capacity for understanding the related things as existing independently of the interests of the perceiving organism]. And when it is said that relations of the sorts in question are not in any way sensible directly or indirectly, the answer is that directly they are not anything thus sensible nor are they formally sensible, but they are indeed sensible fundamentally, insofar as they are founded in those sensible individuals, as, for example, inimicality-to-a-sheep is founded in the nature and qualities of a wolf." – "Non cognosci relationes a sensu interno sub proprio modo relationis, scilicet cum comparatione ad terminum vel discursu neque in universali, sed ut se tenent ex parte fundamenti seu ut exercentur in illo, non ut in actu signato et secundum se relatio potest apprehendi. Fundamentum autem est res ipsa sensibilis prout convenientiam vel disconvenientiam fundat. Sic autem non sentitur a sensu externo, quia illud fundare convenientiam vel disconvenientiam non est color vel

Then, since signs as such – as distinct from their vehicles, interpretants, and significates – consist in relations, the consequence is that, as Maritain put it, such animals as have available only zoösemiotic means of structuring the perceived make use signs within perception without knowing that there are signs. They are absorbed in the objective world without any possibility of developing an understanding of its independent structures beyond and underlying the biological requirements of interaction therewith. For purely perceptual animals, objective world and environment are one. They have no means of knowing that much of the Umwelt is constituted by relations introduced by the mind itself as it elaborates sensory impressions into perceived structures of objectivity. For they have no means of separating the sign as consisting in relation, which yields the objects of experience, from the objects yielded. The apparently unified way in which objects are given in sense perception conceals the profound differences between things in their own right which have been in part objectified and those other aspects of the perceived object which have been introduced on the basis of the organism's own needs and desires, both individual and social. The relations are given with and by the objects experienced, but the animal lacks the means to distinguish the relations from their terms by seeing the difference between mind-dependent and mind-independent elements in the structure of the Umwelt.

The problem of the difference between perception as such (purely zoösemiotic apprehension) and perception suffused with understanding (anthroposemiosis), then, goes to the fact that relations as such are not sense-perceptible. This non-sensory, imperceptible dimension introduced into the structures of objectivity, whether from the physical surroundings or by

sonum aut odor vel aliquid, quod sensu externo percipitur, ipsa tamen relatio ut condistincta a fundamento et ut comparative accepta ad terminum non attingitur per aestimativam sine collatione. Et cum dicitur, quod tales relationes non sunt aliquo modo sensibiles per se vel per accidens, respondetur, quod directe non sunt aliquod tale sensibile nec formaliter, bene tamen fundamentaliter, quatenus in illis fundantur, sicut in natura et qualitatibus lupi fundatur contrarietas ad ovem." See further in this chapter note 30, p. 103 f. below.

the mind's own workings, is wholly transparent to every
external and internal channel of sensation except in its results,
which are the objects structured within perception.[13] Thus the

---

[13] *Tractatus de Signis*, First Preamble, Article 1, 54/29–55/6: "The
response to this [i.e., the objection that privation and negation
bespeak a lack of a form and denominate a subject deficient apart
from any mind's considering; therefore they are not fictive deficien-
cies nor constructed (mind-dependent) beings] is that negation, as
bespeaking the lack of a form, is given on the side of mind-independent being negatively, because the form itself is not in the thing.
Yet it is not called a mind-dependent being for this reason, but
because, while in the physical world it is not a being, but the absence
of a form, it is understood by the understanding [or in perception, for
that matter] after the manner of a being, and so prior to the consideration of the understanding it denominates a deficient subject. But this
deficiency or lack is not properly a formal effect, nor is to remove a
form some form, but the deficiency is understood in the manner of a
formal effect, inasmuch as it is understood in the mode of a form, and
consequently after the pattern of a formal effect, while in fact the deficiency or lack in question is not a formal effect, but the removal of
that effect. And similarly there is an extrinsic denomination on the
part of mind-independent being as regards the denominating form.
But because its application to the thing denominated is not mind-
independently in the very thing denominated, therefore to conceive
that form as adjoining and applied to the very thing denominated is
something mind-dependent [whether in perception or understand-
ing]. But to be a predicate and subject, superior and inferior, is found
prior to the awareness of understanding only fundamentally, not formally under the concept of relation, as will be explained at greater
length in treating of universals." – "Respondetur [ad propositionem
quod privatio et negatio nullo intellectu considerante dicunt carentiam formae et denominant subiectum carens; ergo non sunt carentiae
fictae nec entia rationis] negationem, ut dicit carentiam formae, dari
a parte rei negative, quia ipsa forma in re non est. Non tamen ex hoc
dicitur ens rationis, sed quia cum in re non sit ens, sed carentia formae, accipitur ab intellectu [vel ab sensibus interioribus, i.e., in per-
ceptione] per modum entis, et ita ante considerationem intellectus
[vel etiam in animalem carentem intellectum] denominat subiectum
carens. Sed ista carentia proprie non est effectus formalis, nec tollere
formam est aliqua forma, sed per modum effectus formalis accipitur
ab intellectu, quatenus per modum formae accipitur, et consequenter
ad modum effectus formalis, cum in re illa carentia non sit effectus
formalis, sed ablatio illius. Et similiter denominatio extrinseca a parte
rei datur quantum ad formam denominantem. Sed quia applicatio

animals know, in purely zoösemiotic perception, mind-dependent aspects added to physical objects as if the added aspects were part of the objects' physical being, as if the added aspects were individuating characteristics ("inherent accidents") of that object, without discriminating between what has been added and what was prejacent.

Indeed, if we distinguish sharply between physical individuality, which alone has *inherent accidents* properly speaking, and objective individuality, the "characteristics" added within an objectification by the terminations of mind-dependent relations appear and function as in fact "individuating characteristics" of the objective unity as such. They function to individuate objects within the objective order regardless of their subjective status (or lack thereof) outside the objective order. Whence the "naturalness" of the Umwelt for each animal, since that is the reality of experience at once partially including the physical environment and, at the same time, transcending and reorganizing that included part within a larger objective whole. Comparisons made in perceptual apprehensions suffice to give rise to mind-dependent objectivities even if not to make them recognizable as such, because the relations carried by and necessary to these objective formations never form *as such* a part of the perceptual grasp, by reason of their lacking as such the external aspect of something sensible. Even so, indirectly, if not always in their foundations at least in their terminations as distinct from themselves, they have that external aspect on which sense perception wholly depends. This is the reason why, as we discussed

eius ad rem denominatam non est realiter in ipsa re denominata, ideo concipere illam formam ut adiacentem et applicatam ipsi rei denominatae, aliquid rationis [i.e., mentis] est. Esse autem praedicatum et subiectum, superius et inferius, ante cognitionem intellectus [ut in casu animalium sine intellectu sed capax percipiendi] solum invenitur fundamentaliter, non formaliter sub conceptu relationis, ut latius dicetur agendo de universalibus."

This text is speaking of the understanding, but, as the interpolations in square brackets indicate, it is one of those texts which applies also to perception, as should be clear also from our earlier notes bearing on this point.

earlier in this chapter,[14] recognition of objective relations as such requires quite another sort of comparison than the perceptual comparison by which sensible aspects of the environment objectified in sensation are perceived with the addition within the objectification of mind-dependent aspects undiscriminated from the physical.

Bear in mind that the objective world, without *appearing* so, is through and through relational at all points other than the physical termini of its constitutive relations in the environment. The profound reason for this lies in the very nature of objective being as constituted through a relation to a cognitive organism as such. In the physical environment, there are individuals (substances, in Aristotle's sense) with their identifying characteristics (accidents, in Aristotle's sense), and these latter characteristics, as modifications of substance (the "subject of physical individual existence", actual or possible), are of two sorts. There are those which modify the subject in its subjectivity (inherent accidents); and there are those which, though based or founded upon subjective characteristics whence they provenate, yet *exist* over and above the subjective existence of the individual, and connect it with other individuals and events within the environment (the accident of physical relations, as such dyadic and intersubjective, though virtually triadic and semiosic, as we saw in the last chapter).[15] This situation needs to be examined in careful detail.

The objective world is constituted unto itself, in principle, by the single rationale of intersubjectivity. The physical environment, by contrast, exhibits a twofold rationale of being: *subjectivity*, both substantial and accidental, and *intersubjectivity*, only accidental though essential to the existence and

---

[14] P. 78 and following.

[15] We should also note that, already as early as Aristotle (4th century BC), we find a thematic awareness that the very framework of the physical insofar as animals actively situate themselves within it already expresses an irreducible collusion of mind and nature even in such anthroposemiotic "categories" as space, time, position, protective guises: see "The basic categorial scheme and its details" in Chapter 3 of Deely 2001: 74 ff.

survival of substances through the constant dependence of individuals on definite ranges of environmental conditions in their initial coming into existence and no less in their ongoing being. Cognition, or "mind" (the capacity of some living substances to become partially aware of their surroundings through objectification) is the source of relations as cognitive, and some of these, we have seen, in perception as well as in sensation, are in part identical with physical relations of the environment. But such physical relations as such as are subsumed and resumed within cognition (within the structure of the objective world) become, through that subsumption, triadic, and hence no longer dependent for their existence as relations on the physical existence of their objective terminus (even though they continue to so depend in order to be physical *as well as* objective).

The mind thus introduces relations into the objective world in two ways: by incorporating into cognition relations that are there in the physical surroundings, and by adding to these relations further relations of its own devising. Since the relations already there in the physical environment, even as subsumed within the net of sensations, have no per se sensible content of themselves and directly, whatever relations are subsumed within sensation or are added to the sensory core by the activities of perception remain transparent even to perception. Be it noted that, except in their diverse foundations and terminations, as such "subjective" (i.e., characteristics of individuals of whatever sort at least objectively, whether or not also subjectively[16]), in comparison to the "intersubjectivity" of the relations themselves according to the way they have their proper being as relations (which is the ground of the invisibility of the ordering whereby the objects of experience have the de facto individuation and arrangement according to which they appear to whatever organism as they appear), *all* the relations of sense perceptions, those which are

---

[16] Hence the quotation marks around the term "subjective" in the modified clause.

physical as well as objective and those which have being only in the arrangement of the objective world or Umwelt, remain transparent to sense. Indirectly only, through their foundations and termini, are they sensed, not as such but as the structure or pattern of objectivity, the "related objects" of experience and the "characteristics" of whatever "objects" are given in perception.

When cognition creates or forms relations that have being only in the objective world, therefore, if the cognition is purely zoösemiotic (perceptual only), these relations *appear* only indirectly, not as relations, but (through their foundations and terminations) *as* characteristics of objects related. The only relations formed by cognition itself that are apprehended *as* relations are those that are understood in contrast to whatever foundation and terminus they connect. But this is also true of relations in the physical environment: the only relations formed at the level of brute secondness that are apprehended *as* relations are those that come to be understood in contrast to whatever foundation and terminus they connect. By contrast, the foundation and the terminus, when they belong to the order of sense, are directly both intelligible and sensible; hence they can be both understood and perceived. But even when the foundation and the terminus belong to the sensory order, the relation between them is directly intelligible but only indirectly sensible. Whence the fact that relations as such are in no case sense-perceptible.

Hence when the mind, whether in perception or understanding, forms relations by objectively comparing any two or more things which belong or appear to belong to the subjective order (individual substances with their subjective characteristics), the relations which result, being relations, *are not* what their compared terms are, namely, instances belonging to the rationale of subjectivity. Such mind-dependent relations were called by the Latins *"negationes"*, negations, in view of this situation – the situation that they are not what their compared terms appear as. Existing only comparatively to what they are not, they are named not from what they are (namely, relations), but from the fact that they are not that to which they are compared (namely, a substance or an inherent accident). Only these mind-dependent relations, so-called *negations* by contrast with the positive types of subjectivity to which they are compared, are formed in a purely zoösemiotic apprehension.

By contrast, the understanding alone grasps the intelligible content of relation as having a being in opposition to its foundations and termini. The *relatio secundum esse*, the being proper to relations according to what they are as such, the suprasubjectivity which they enjoy according to the way they have being whether realized in the physical and objective orders or only in the objective order, is directly understood (or at least understandable), whether indirectly sensed or not sensed at all (as in the case of grammatical, logical, or mathematical relations). When the understanding forms on its own relations patterned after the being proper to relations, to the at most indirectly sensible connections of foundations and termini conceived as such, what the mind then forms is the very thing that can also be realized independently of the mind, namely, a relation as such. The fact that only some of the relations created by thought, and those only sometimes, can find the physical circumstances requisite for them to occur as physical relations is quite beside this point.

For it remains that the understanding is able to form something on the pattern of physical relations given in sensation understood as the intersubjective connection between foundation and terminus, distinguished as such both from the foundation (a subjective characteristic) and from the terminus (also a subjective characteristic). *This* basis for forming mind-dependent relations, since it cannot be directly perceived through sense, is never available for the imitative and comparative formation in pure perception of further relations. When perception adds to relations of sensation yet further relations, thus, it does so without ever realizing that it is doing so. Exactly what it is doing perception has not the wherewithall to thematize. It forms only what, from the point of view of understanding, would be recognized as so-called

"negations".[17] These negations, being purely objective relations, have strictly speaking no subjective termini as such in
the subjective order of physical being. Yet their termini, even
though purely objective, imitate the appearance of subjective
characteristics. Through this imitation they individuate
objects differently than whatever those objects have of physical being is individuated as physical. The two orders – the
physical order of the environment and the objective order of
the experienced world – are internally differentiated according to quite different principles of organization, despite their
partial coincidences and overlaps often verified by the success
of hunters and the survival of species, as well as by the critical control of objectification in which science consists.

Understanding adds to this difference in the organization
of the physical and the objective. It does so not only by the creation of further relations in the class of negations but also by
consciously and explicitly adding relations as such, relations
of its own devising recognized and known from the first to be
relations as distinct from the foundations and termini through
the correlation of which all relations have their proper being –
including those other mind-dependent (or purely objective)
relations, the *negationes*. These last mind-dependent relations,
for the reasons we have seen, are not called what they in fact
are, namely, relations, but are named rather after their foundations and termini which, were it a case of physical relations,
would have a positive being in physical subjectivity as inherent accidents of substance, but which, since it is a case not

---

[17] This name, which the Latins assigned to the group of cognition-
dependent relations that, through their foundations and termini, are
capable of contributing to the way in which the objective world
appears differently in its units and divisions of being than are the
units and divisions of being in the physical universe as such, strikes
me as opaque in consequence of its overly-compressed rationale of
assignment; but there is for the moment no way to take account of the
traditional development of this point bearing on semiotic without
making use of the term, for which I otherwise apologize to my read-
ers.

only of objective relations but of *merely and exclusively* objective relations, are the mere "negatives" of such inherent accidents, objective appearances without subjective physical counterpart. These relations, so-called "negations", and only some of them, alone as mind-dependent relations are found on both sides of the intersemiosis of perception and understanding.

We are now at a point where we can make explicit a proposition that does not reach a fully explicit formulation in any Latin text known to me, even though it was just below the surface, so to speak, of the texts constituting the *Tractatus de Signis* that I found it. To speak more directly, as an immediate consequence of what is explicitly said in the *Tractatus de Signis*, the following proposition is implicit: *all* purely objective or "mind-dependent" being, though only some physical being, is in principle intersubjective, as should appear from the following considerations.

The physical order has the twofold rationale of subjectivity and intersubjectivity, but the objective order, in whatever is contributed to it by the workings of mind alone, is purely intersubjective as a matter of principle. Even in those cases where this intersubjectivity is not achieved as a matter of fact (e.g., when some individual has dreamed up something new, whether an invention that could be realized or some fantastic animal, but has as yet shared the creation with no one else), the purely relational constructs of objectivity exist suprasubjectively, and hence as *capable*, under the right circumstances, of being communicated so as to realize in fact an intersubjective condition or state.

To help grasp the point so abstractly stated, simply think of any message you have decided to give to another as it exists in the secrecy of your mind prior to being communicated. At that point it is suprasubjective in fact – it exists as known, and therefore at the terminus of a set of cognitive relations rather than subjectively as merely part of your "psychology" – but not yet in fact as intersubjective, since you are the only subject in possession of the knowledge. As soon as you convey the message (say, a proposal to marry), what was intersubjective

in principle becomes intersubjective in fact, a point of information to which two subjects are related in common. (For the
example to work, of course, the proposal in this case must
come as a surprise and not have been given away in advance
even zoösemiotically. This is not often the case; and, when it is
the case, increases the risk of refusal. Such are life's chances.)

In summary, from the proposition that "there are only two
kinds of mind-dependent being",[18] it follows as an immediate
consequence that all mind-dependent beings are essentially
relations according to the ways relations have being. For the
exhaustive and exclusive traditional division of mind-
dependent being into negations and relations is not based
upon a difference in the final outcome of cognitive activity
whenever it gives rise to constructions having only objective
being.[19] The division is drawn rather from the basis in experience from which the mind, in achieving that final outcome,
acts in view of:[20] in the case of negations, some being or feature of being intrinsically subjective ("substance", i.e., a physical individual, or any "inhering accident", i.e., an individual
characteristic); in the case of relations, that unique feature of
being which serves only to connect individuals with what is
other than themselves (with other subjectivities or objectivities
which they themselves are not) and so exists suprasubjectively

---

[18] *Tractatus de Signis*, First Preamble, Article 1, 51/38–41: "St. Thomas
exhaustively divides mind-dependent being into two members,
namely, into *negation* and mind-dependent *relation*" – "Id, inquit,
quod est rationis, non potest esse nisi duplex, scilicet, negatio vel aliqua relatio."

[19] *Tractatus de Signis*, First Preamble, Article 3, 69/14–18 (I add the italics): "every mind-dependent being is either a relation or some negation. If a relation, it must be apprehended *comparatively to a term*. If a
negation, it must be conceived positively on the pattern of being,
which is to be conceived *comparatively to another*." – "omne ens rationis vel est relatio vel aliqua negatio. Si relatio, *debet comparative apprehendi ad terminum*. Si negatio, debet concipi positive ad instar entis,
quod est *comparative ad alterum*." Q.E.D.

[20] See the First Preamble "On Mind-Dependent Being," Article 1 "What
in general a mind-dependent being is and how many kinds there are"
in *Tractatus de Signis*, 48–57, esp. 51/29–53/45 and 56/1–57/30.

(and intersubjectively in fact whenever the patterning relation is physical, which it need not be, whence the infinity of semiosis[21]).

"Negations" are relations which exist only from a comparative cognitive activity undertaken in view of the occasionally directly sensible aspects of relations characterizing individuals, namely, the foundations and termini of relations. As *distinguished from negations, however,* there are yet other mind-dependent relations which, like negations, exist only from cognitive activity, but, unlike negations, are taken in view of the never directly sensible aspects of relations according to which relations are precisely constituted suprasubjectively in their proper and unique being as relations and not merely characterized indirectly through a "subject" (or some individualized object), whether as founding or terminating the relation. *These* mind-dependent beings not only *are* relations (as also are negations), but, being themselves what also are their exemplars in the intellectual objectification of the physical environment, were as well *called* "relations" by the Latins.

But when the Latins wished to emphasize not the contrast of objective constructions to the objectified physical being of the environment as it partially intrudes itself through experience into the Umwelt, but rather the indifference of relation in its proper being to the question of whether its subjective source or ground in any given case is the mind, on one hand, or physical nature, on the other, then they spoke not of "negations" in contrast to "relations", but simply in terms of *relatio secundum esse*, relation according to the way it has being. For this designation included and applied to alike physical relations and objective relations, those objective relations which were at the same time physical as well as those objective

---

[21] See *Tractatus de Signis*, First Preamble, Article 2, esp. 61/37–62/18. The whole matter of infinite process, both as a physical process among causes and as an objective process among relations, is discussed at length in Deely 1994, the only such treatment I know of. See also the neat summary formulation of the source of infinity among the relations of the objective world, cited below on p. 122 f.

relations which have no other than objective being, whether capable of being formed zoösemiotically as well as anthroposemiotically (the case of the mind-dependent relations called "negations") or capable of being formed only anthroposemiotically (the case of the mind-dependent relations called "relations").

And when they wished to emphasize the contrast of all pure relations to the subjective being according to which the physical environment and the psychology of individuals exists in and through a potentially infinite series of interactions and interdependencies, they spoke of the *relativum secundum dici*, the transcendentally relative, in contrast to the *relationes secundum esse*, the ontologically pure cases of relation. These pure cases are the ones that are indifferently objective only or physical as well as objective (or even hypothetically physical only in some region or level of the universe as yet untouched by the expansion of human experience and understanding that we call today positive science).

As opposed to negations, mind-dependent relations, the pure objectivities existing only in and through the activity of understanding (intellectual semiosis) in its difference from perception, are relations formed by the understanding on the bases of the never directly sensible aspects of relations precisely in their proper suprasubjectivity, the aspect proper to them as such and not merely indirectly through a subject. But the fact that relations are formed as such by the understanding in its proper objective dimension should not blind us to the further fact that directly sensible aspects of relations, namely, the material individuals and aspects of individuals on which relations are founded and at which relations terminate, can *also* be relatively recombined in perception as well as in intellection to form objects other than what is physically present to sensation as such. And patterns of relations formed in this way, *negations as opposed to strictly anthroposemiosic mind-dependent relations*, are no less relations according to their proper being than are either the physical relations themselves exemplified in experience or the mind-dependent relations the understanding forms expressly as such.

>93<

To speak of negations *and* relations formed by the mind, thus, can be – and, historically, virtually without exception has been – profoundly misleading. For both negations and relations formed by the mind are relations according to the way they have being. It is just that the basis from which the latter are formed is accessible only to the understanding in its difference from sense perception, while the basis from which the former are formed is accessible to sensation and perception as well as to human understanding.

We should say more simply, and with far less chance of confusion and misunderstanding, that relations may result either from the mind or from nature, and many relations arising from the one source may be so transposed in their foundations as to exist also from the other source. But when relations exist from the mind they may arise either from the mind's considering rationales of subjectivity merely or from considering rationales of intersubjectivity as well, in the former case giving rise to objective structures zoösemiotically as well as anthroposemiotically, in the latter case giving rise to objective structures only anthroposemiotically. In either case, the objective structures in whatever of them is purely objective exist only in, through, and as relations or sets and networks of relations, whereas in the physical environment, including that part of it which occasionally intrudes through sensation into the objective world, there are subjectively existing individuals with their subjective characteristics, as well as relations among individuals.

All objective unities exist at least as intersections of relations; those objective unities that also exist subjectively do so from the side of physical, not from the side of purely objective, being. But because all objective unities as such have the same constitution of relative being, only experiment and experience can enable us to tell when our objects possess a subjective dimension in their objectivity and when we are only dreaming (for "man has many sleeps", as Maritain put it). Between these limit cases there are many degrees, degrees which form the fabric of human life and civilization in particular.

Bearing in mind what was mentioned above about essences consisting in relational models insofar as they have an objective being,[22] we are now in a position to explain better, or at least more clearly, than Cajetan did himself explain his claim that "a rose formed by the mind is not a rose, though a relation formed by the mind is a relation".[23] For just as a relation formed by the mind is a relation, so is a rose formed by the mind a relation. That is what the mind does: form relations; and, of itself, nothing besides, though the relations it forms may often be transferred into the physical or the cultural environment through an appropriate control exercised over material conditions.

Imagine yourself to chance on a meadow where a wild rose grows. The rose in the meadow exists subjectively, as does its characteristic shape. When you chance on it, what existed subjectively acquires also a relation to you thanks to which it begins to exist objectively as well. The next afternoon

[22] See p. 71 ff. above. Further discussion in Deely 1994, beginning at ¶296.

[23] From Cajetan's *Commentary* (1507 publication date) on the *Summa Theologiae*, I, q. 28, art. 1, 9: "Relation is the sort of being for which the qualification existing in the mind does not detract from what is proper to it, as it does detract from what is proper to all other sorts of being. For a rose formed by thought is not a rose, nor is Homer in the mind's consideration Homer; but a relation formed by the mind is a true relation . . . Nor is the distinction between a rose in natural existence and in intellectual existence a distinction of two diverse things, of which the one is a mind-independent being and the other a mind-dependent being, as we have said happens in the case of relation: but it is a distinction of one and the same thing according to different modes of existing, namely, absolutely or relatively." – "relatio est tale ens, cui additum esse in ratione non est conditio diminuens, sicut in aliis. Rosa enim secundum rationem, non est rosa; neque Homerus in opinione, est Homerus; relatio autem in ratione, est vera relatio. . . . Nec distinctio rosae in esse naturae et esse rationis, est distinctio diversarum quidditatum, quarum una sit ens reale, et altera sit ens rationis, ut in relatione contingere diximus: sed est distinctio unius et eiusdem secundum diversos modos essendi, scilicet simpliciter vel secundum quid."

you take a friend to see this beautiful wild rose, only to discover that in the morning the meadow had been plowed and the rose destroyed. The rose, formerly existing subjectively as well as objectively, exists now only objectively, and – insofar as your friend· has shared from your conversations in an awareness of the rose that was (for the one who plowed the meadow had taken no notice, and no one besides you had passed that way since the rose first bloomed) – intersubjectively.

The rose in your thought was not a substance but an object, that is to say, a pattern of relations. Indeed, the rose too in the meadow was made possible only through a series of relations which, when sufficiently altered, involved the destruction of the rose; but the rose in the meadow was not, was other than, those physical relations which contributed to its existence: it was a subjectively existing individual, a "substance", if you like. Its shape was not just a distinctive pattern of relationships, but a subjective characteristic, an "inherent accident", if you like. In your remembrance, the rose as an object existed only through a pattern of relations, of which its distinctive shape formed a part, but without that further subjective dimension which gave the rose in the meadow the more than objective existence of a physical subjectivity. The physical subjectivity as such was indeed directly objectified when you first beheld the rose and it acted on your eyes through some of the physical relations which were part of its circumstances in the meadow. But the objectification itself, as capable of surviving the subjectivity, consisted in a set of relations according to the being proper to relation, whereby it is indifferent to whether its ground is in physical nature alone, cognitive activity alone, or both physical nature and cognitive activity together. The rose in thought is a relation, but of the sort that would be a negation had the rose been formed by imagination alone. The rose in the meadow is a substance, existing only on the presupposition of various relations and other things, but in itself something other than what it presupposes (what it is transcendentally relative to) for physical continuance.

What is *excluded* from the objective order in its contrast with the physical environment as such, thus, is the rationale of subjectivity in all its parts:

> that on whose pattern a mind-dependent being is formed is not called mind-dependent, for mind-dependent being is formed on the pattern of mind-independent being; but that unreal being which is conceived on the pattern of a mind-independent being is called a mind-dependent being. There is not therefore mind-dependent substance nor mind-dependent quantity, because even though some non-being may be conceived on the pattern of a substance – for example, the chimera – and some on the pattern of quantity – for example, imaginary space – yet neither substance itself nor any rationale of subjectivity is conceived by the understanding and formed in being on the pattern of some other mind-independent being.[24]

[24] *Tractatus de Signis*, Second Preamble, Article 2, 96/7–19. "And for this reason," the text continues (96/19–28), "that negation or chimerical non-being and that non-being of an imaginary space will be said to be a mind-dependent being. But this [i.e., any unreal object whatever conceived as being a subject or a subjective modification of being] is the mind-dependent being which is called negation, yet it will not be a mind-dependent substance, because substance itself is not conceived as a mind-dependent being patterned after some mind-independent being – rather, negations or non-beings are conceived on the pattern of substance and quantity."

This whole text, *Tractatus de Signis*, Second Preamble, Article 2, 96/7–28, reads in the original as follows: "non dicitur ens rationis illud, ad cuius instar formatur; formatur enim ens rationis ad instar entis realis, sed dicitur ens rationis illud non reale, quod ad instar realis entis concipitur. Non datur ergo substantia rationis nec quantitas rationis, quia licet aliquod non ens concipiatur ad instar substantiae, v. g. chimaera, et aliquid ad instar quantitatis, v. g. spatium imaginarium, non tamen ipsa substantia vel aliqua substantiae ratio concipitur per rationem et formatur in esse ad instar alterius entis realis. Et ideo illa negatio seu non ens chimaerae, et illud non ens spatii imaginarii dicetur ens rationis. Sed hoc est ens rationis, quod

What is *included* in the objective order, *even in its contrast with the physical order as such and hence as their area of overlap*, is the rationale of the intersubjective:

> But in the case of relatives, indeed, not only is there some non-being conceived on the pattern of relation, but also the very relation conceived on the part of the respect toward, while it does not exist in the mind-independent order, is conceived or formed on the pattern of a mind-independent relation, and so that which is formed in being, and not only that after whose pattern it is formed, is a relation, and by reason of this there are in fact mind-dependent relations, but not mind-dependent substances.[25]

But – and on this point hangs the whole of semiosis – as a result of its being constituted in its proper being exclusively according to the rationale of the intersubjective, the objective order *cannot be completely separated from the universe of physical being*.[26] Psychosis is possible, yes. But a capsule of consciousness

vocatur negatio, non autem erit substantia rationis, cum non ipsa substantia ut ens rationis ad instar alicuius realis concipiatur, sed negationes seu non entia ad instar substantiae et quantitatis."

[25] *Tractatus de Signis*, Second Preamble, Article 2, 96/28–36: "At vero in relativis non solum aliquod non ens concipitur ad instar relationis, sed etiam ipsa relatio ex parte respectus ad, cum non existit in re, concipitur seu formatur ad instar relationis realis, et sic est, quod formatur in esse, et non solum id, ad cuius instar formatur, et ratione huius datur relatio rationis, non substantia rationis."

[26] *Tractatus de Signis*, Book I, Question 2: 149/41–151/21: "the rationale of something knowable and of an object can be univocal in a mind-independent and in a mind-dependent being; for the divisions of being in the order of physical existence are one thing, while divisions in the order of the knowable are quite another, as Cajetan well teaches in Part I, q. 1, art. 3, of his *Commentary* on the *Summa Theologica*. And so the rationale of something knowable is not the rationale of being formally, but only presuppositively is it being and consequent upon being; for the true is a coincident property of being, and so formally is not being, but consequent upon being and presuppositively being; but the true is the same as the knowable. Whence it can well

incapable in principle of assimilating to itself and presenting
as such also the being proper to the physical environment in

be that some being incapable of [mind-independent] existence is
capable of truth, not as a subject, but as an object, inasmuch as it does
not have in itself the entitative being which as subject founds truth
and knowability, but does have that which as object can be known
after the pattern of mind-independent being and so exist objectively
in the understanding as something true. Whence, although entita-
tively mind-independent being and mind-dependent being are
analogized, nevertheless, objectively, because the one is represented
on the pattern of the other, even beings which are not univocal enti-
tatively can coincide in a univocal rationale of an object, as, for example, God and the creature, substance and accident in the rationale of
a metaphysical knowable, or of something understandable by the
human mind. Moreover, the rationale of a sign, because it does not
consist absolutely in the rationale of an object, but of a substitution
for another which is supposed to be the object or thing signified, that
it may be represented to a cognitive power, does not pertain to the
order of the cognizable absolutely, but relatively and ministerially;
and for this role the rationale of a sign takes on something of the entitative order, to wit, as it is a relation and as it draws the order of the
knowable to the order of the relative, and for this function a natural
sign-relation, which is mind-independent, does not coincide univo-
cally with a stipulated sign-relation, which is mind-dependent." –
"ratio cognoscibilis et obiecti in ente reali et rationis potest esse univoca; aliae enim sunt divisiones entis in esse rei, aliae in genere scibilis, ut bene Caietanus docet 1. p. q. 1. art. 3. Et sic ratio cognoscibilis
non est ratio entis formaliter, sed praesuppositive solum est ens et
consecutum ad ens; verum enim est passio entis, et sic formaliter non
est ens, sed consecutum ad ens et praesuppositive ens; idem est
autem verum quod cognoscibile. Unde bene stat, quod aliquod ens
incapax existentiae sit capax veritatis, non ut subiectum, sed ut obiectum, quatenus non habet in se entitatem, quae tamquam subiectum
fundet veritatem et cognoscibilitatem, sed habet, quod tamquam
obiectum possit cognosci ad instar entis realis et sic obiective esse in
intellectu tamquam verum. Unde licet entitative ens reale et ens rationis analogentur, tamen obiective, cum unum ad instar alterius
repraesentetur, possunt in ratione univoca obiecti convenire etiam
quae entitative univoca non sunt, ut Deus et creatura, substantia et
accidens in ratione scibilis metaphysici vel intelligibilis ab intellectu.
Ceterum ratio signi cum non consistat in ratione obiecti absolute, sed
substitutionis ad alterum, quod supponitur esse obiectum seu signatum, ut repraesentetur potentiae, non pertinet ad genus cognoscibilis

whatever it has that is prejacent to or independent of human thought and action – the situation envisaged by the moderns and systematized so brilliantly by Immanuel Kant – is a chimera on a footing with the Chimaera of Greek mythology: a mind-dependent being with, indeed, a foundation in reality, as Suárez might have said, but a mind-dependent being none-theless, a creation which is not what its foundation is, namely, a situation existing in fact.

By its proper constitution in principle according to the rationale of intersubjectivity, the objective order and the physical order partially overlap and interpenetrate one anoth-er in the life of organisms through semiosis. Indeed, just this

absolute, sed relative et ministerialiter; et pro hac parte aliquid enti-tativi ordinis induit, scilicet ut relatio est et ut trahit genus cognosci-bilis ad genus relativi, et pro hac parte non convenit univoce relatio signi naturalis, quae realis est, cum relatione signi ad placitum, quae est rationis."

This last point, on the different ways in which sign-vehicles work when they are intrinsically connected with the relations they support (for example, as smoke relates to fire) and when (for example, as the English word "smoke" relates to smoke) they are only extrinsically connected with their sign-vehicle by a stipulation (*signum ad plac-itum*) or even a habit structure (*signum ex consuetudine*) having, how-ever, no existence apart from the Lebenswelt or Unwelt in its purely objective being, bears particular noting. It is the difference between *motivated* and *arbitrary* signs, in one contemporary way of speaking, which the Latins expressed by distinguishing the natural sign from the conventional sign. The text of the *Tractatus de Signis* again and again manifests that on the understanding of this difference depends one's answer to the question of whether such a thing as a unified doc-trine of signs is possible (see, e.g., Book II, Question 1, 235/36–236/42, and Question 5). In the end, the manner in which natural and stipulated signs work differently in the making known of the physi-cal universe (the partial drawing of it into the objective order, asymp-totically expanded by the dialectic of scientific instruments and theo-ries), even though in the objective order they are univocal (that is, signs in exactly the same sense), is what provides the justification of experiment in science, and the reason why all attempts based on the authority of texts, sacred no less than secular, to decide issues that fall within experience are vain exercises in folly (to which, unfortunately, the history of our species manifests we have been only too prone).

interpenetration is what we call experience, just this interpenetration is what constitutes the objective world.

The whole of semiosis hangs on this point[27] because the action of signs is rooted in the being proper to signs, and only through the action proper to signs – *semiosis,* as we say – does the objective world achieve in the experience of organisms the full actuality of its difference from the mere physical being of the environment, what Eddington called so elegantly "the physical world".

By virtue of the suprasubjective constitution of the objective world, it not only consists in a network of relations, but this network itself is a constantly shifting mix, a flux, of mind-dependent and mind-independent relations (purely objective relations and objective relations which are also physical), where what is at one moment mind-dependent can be at the next moment mind-independent, and vice-versa. But perception at every moment is aware only of foundations and termini of those relations, never of the relations themselves, and hence has no way to discriminate between what is mind-independent and what mind-dependent within and among its objects.

Human and other animals are alike in transforming objects of sensation into objects perceived according to the needs, desires, and customs of the perceiver. They do this by adding to the sensory impressions such further relations as will proportion what is sensed to those desiderata. But *further to recognize* the relativity of such additions to their source and their comparative nonbeing in the destination – the object perceived – requires the *further capacity* to grasp the difference between relation itself, as something *nonsensible but obtaining* between aspects of objects, and the sensible aspects of the objects as such related which give rise to, without themselves being, the relations. This further capacity is the formal root of the difference between "sense" and "intellect".

---

[27] And, inasmuch as semiotics is the knowledge that results from thematizing and inquiring into the action of signs, we could equally say that upon the point in question hangs the whole of semiotics.

Hence, of the two sorts of pure objectivities which have formal existence only in apprehension – those called "negations", which are patterned after subjective characteristics of physical being; and those called "relations", which are patterned after intersubjective aspects of physical being[28] – both in fact, inasmuch as they consist in a "being patterned after", are essentially relations according to the way they have being, which is to say always suprasubjectively in fact and in principle intersubjectively as well.[29] So-called negations are *patterned after* subjective aspects of physical being objectified directly by sense. But purely objective relations are *patterned after* intersubjective aspects of physical being objectified, which aspects cannot be sensed directly but only indirectly in their foundations and terminations, comparatively subjective aspects. From this arise different levels of comparison requisite to form an awareness of the two, as we saw earlier in this chapter. For the former, the formation of negations, which are purely objective relations but are not envisaged as such in the process of their formation, sense perception suffices. But for the latter, the formation of purely objective relations envisaged

[28] See *Tractatus de Signis*, First Preamble, Article 1, 51/27–52/8 and 53/9–45.

[29] Hence the profundity of the assertion in the *Tractatus de Signis*, explaining the Latinized Greek title "Perihermenias" (38/21–39/4), that the success of an inquiry into the nature of the sign depends principally upon the understanding of purely objective or mind-dependent being and the nature of relation as verified in the order of mind-independent or physical being objectified: "these questions about signs . . . may be authentically introduced in this work, following a consideration of mind-dependent being and of the category of relation [as a type of physical reality], on which considerations this inquiry concerning the nature and definable essence of signs principally depends" – "quaestiones istae de signis . . . in hoc loco genuine introducuntur, post notitiam habitam de ente rationis et praedicamento relationis, a quibus principaliter dependet inquisitio ista de natura et quidditate signorum" (cf. Deely 1977).

For the reason for the location of the *Tractatus de Signis* text both within the *Ars Logica* as a part and within the traditional *Cursus Philosophicus* as a whole expression of the then-traditional "curriculum of arts", see initially 38/1–20 in the *Tractatus de Signis*, and Deely 1994a: 65–105.

as such, since no directly sensory pattern is involved, sense perception can gain no purchase. Whence mind-dependent relations *as such* remain forever invisible to sense perception, while mind-dependent relations *as negations*, even though they too are essentially mind-dependent relations *secundum esse eorum*, appear to sense perception not at all as what they are (pure relations). The objective relations which are negations appear rather only indirectly through their foundations and termini, just as if they were properties of the objects which they structure, on a footing with the subjective characteristics of physical individuals giving rise to relations within sensation in *its* difference from perception (and always remembering that these relations from sensation are incorporated as such within perception along with the addition of its own relations).

Thus, in terms of sensation and perception, each of the features whereby individuality is constituted objectively or *recognized*, except (owing to its diapheneity to sense) relation as such, is directly accessible within a zoösemiotic perception. But only in perception as suffused and transformed from within by the awareness proper to understanding – that is to say, only in anthroposemiosis – is relation itself, in its proper being as suprasubjective, directly accessible.

By way of illustrating these abstract distinctions, let us note that there is a difference – and in this sense perception consists as such – between a certain sound simply as impinging on an auditory receptor and that impingement assimilated to an awareness of danger.[30] But there is quite another difference

---

[30] *Tractatus de Signis*, Book I, Question 6, 214/12–32: ". . . a sheep, when it hears a lion's roar, apprehends the lion as something harmful and as harmful in a specific way, for the sheep flees and fears the roar more because it comes from a lion than if it were the howl of a wolf. Whence the sheep discriminates between the one and the other, which would not be the case if it were not led by means of those signs to a lion and to a wolf as different from one another, and harmful in different ways. The fact that the sheep forms the judgment about the lion and the wolf as things to be fled by a natural instinct, does not remove the fact that the sheep does this from a pre-existing knowledge. For some knowledge in external sense must necessarily pre-

between a profile distinguished by black and white areas, which most any higher animal can well perceive, and the understanding that this perceived pattern is a police car, which no animal without language is able to achieve, even if, on quite other interpretive grounds (purely zoösemiotic), the perceiving animal is frightened by and flees from what it sees in this case.

Perhaps we are now in a position to sketch the anatomy of the distinctively anthroposemiosic competence in which consists the species-specifically human use of signs. It has a skeletal structure of three components. Human animals are able to distinguish between *a sign*, consisting as such in a relationship over and above whatever vehicle (sensible or psychological) may happen to sustain it here and now, and *what it signifies*, the object at which the sign-relation terminates to constitute a signified distinct from the sign. But this apparently simple distinction between sign and signified, so stated, is actually misleading. For in the distinction in fact three irreducible factors are at play. What is being differentiated is, first, the *semiosic relation* in which the sign consists. Then, second, the *vehi-*

cede, either a cognition that sees the lion or one that hears his roar, in order for the estimative sense to apprehend and adjudge the lion as an enemy. For brute animals have judgment, but without indifference, and therefore determined to one thing and based on natural instinct, which instinct does not exclude cognition and judgment, but [only liberty of] indifference. Concerning this point St. Thomas's remarks in the *Summa Theologica*, I, q. 83, art. 1, and in his Disputed Questions on Truth, q. 24, art. 2 can be looked at." – "ovis audito rugitu apprehendit leonem ut nocivum et ut tale nocivum, magis enim fugit et timet rugitum, quia leonis est, quam clamorem lupi. Unde facit discretionem inter unum et aliud, quod non esset, nisi per illa signa duceretur in leonem et in lupum, ut distinguuntur inter se, et diverso modo nociva. Quod autem naturali instinctu formet iudicium de leone et lupo fugiendo, non tollit, quin id fiat ex praeexistente cognitione. Necessario enim in sensu externo debet praecedere aliqua cognitio, vel quae videat leonem vel audiat eius rugitum, ut aestimativa ipsum ut inimicum apprehendat et iudicet. Habent enim bruta iudicium, sed sine indifferentia, ideoque determinatum ad unum et ex instinctu naturali, qui instinctus cognitionem iudiciumque non excludit, sed indifferentiam. De quo videri potest S. Thomas 1. p. q. 83. art. 1. et q. 24. de Veritate art. 2."

cle by which this relation is here and now triggered or conveyed (the sense-perceptible structure or indeed the psychological structure upon which the sign relation is based, whether by reason of the intrinsic constitution of that structure as physical – in the case of psychological states and external natural signs – or by reason of a convention assimilating the particular objective structure to its signification "arbitrarily", without any intrinsic motivation). And finally the *significate* to which the sign-vehicle carries the cognizing organism by way of its cognition, its "content", if you like (the object signified, which understanding can then further discriminate as consisting in various mind-dependent or mind-independent aspects combined). (In the background, as the reason here and now for the connection between sign-vehicle and object as a connection of signification, lies also the *interpretant*; but into this factor here is not the place to delve, since it is a factor generic to *all* semiosis in contrast to the factors species-specifically anthroposemiotic or human.[31])

[31] At just this point did Charles Sanders Peirce pick up the thread of the Latin discussion, and the privilege of assigning a name to the third term of the triadic sign-relation goes to him as marking the decisive advance over late Latin medieval and renaissance (or "early modern") semiotic with which contemporary semiotics begins. For even though the Latin authors had reached the point of explicitly identifying the sign-relation as irreducibly triadic more or less at the very moment when their discussion was doomed to a period of oblivion as the classical modern mainstream authors pursued instead the "way of ideas" (see p. ix above), they had not gotten explicitly beyond the generic, common, and (as would ultimately prove) inadequate, designation of this third term as "mind" or "cognitive power". Yet there are already present in their texts (see Deely 1989) explicit propositions which can be shown to imply that this third term, the then-as-yet-unnamed interpretant, "need not be of a mental mode of being", as Peirce eventually put the matter (c.1906: 5.473). And the absence of this decisive notion needed to explain the connection between sign-vehicle and signified object here and now regardless of the question of whether the sign-vehicle be a "motivated" or an "arbitrary" vehicle, is clearly felt in the seminal text added, so far as we know from the deceased author's own notes or manuscripts, to the 1663 production of the *Tractatus de Signis* (Book I, Question 2, note 4 at 137/7), which I have already quoted in Ch. 5,

Using signs in this species-specific way, the human animal is able to regard the object signified in its own right (albeit fallibly), that is, as it exists or fails to exist apart from the relations through which it is objectified. The ground of this possibility is also the source of what is distinctive in the human use of signs. For it would appear that what is first apprehended intellectually, insofar as intellection differs from perception, is the objective world in relation to itself.[32] In this apprehension the imperceptible "relation to itself" is the sole contribution of understanding. Yet this contribution is sufficient both to elevate the perceptible elements of the Umwelt to the level of intelligibility and, by the same stroke, to transform the generically animal Umwelt into a species-specifically human objective world, a Lebenswelt, an objective world perfused with stipulable signs apprehended as such in the heart of otherwise naturally determined significations.

If this be so, then a neglected insight of the Latin scholastics would appear to be not merely insufficiently understood, but even central for semiotics, namely, their realization that the physical environment, insofar as it enters into the cognitive structure constituting an Umwelt, is of itself sensible but not of itself intelligible. Understanding itself, taking the materials of sensation and perception as its base, has to make that material actually intelligible. The understanding does this by first seeing the whole material of perception – the objective world or Umwelt in all its parts – in relation to itself, over and above the relations to biological needs and interests which are already factored into the structure of the Umwelt by virtue of the evolutionary heritage of the cognitive organism. Hence the objective world, seen in relation to itself, already consists of a mixture of mind-independent and mind-dependent relations undistinguished as such but structuring all particular objects.

note 20, p. 63 f. above. For further indications on this point, see, in the *Tractatus de Signis*, Book I, Question 3, 160/10–21, and the discussion in note 13 of that same Question, pp. 163–64, which still does not rise to the level of explicitly and fully recognizing the interpretant in its unique character.

[32] *See The Human Use of Signs* (Deely 1994), esp. Part IV.

The first action of the understanding is to apprehend its objective world in such a way that its various parts *can eventually* be understood critically, and this is to apprehend the objective world under that mind-dependent relation which allows its contents to appear, truly or falsely, as present-at-hand and not ready-to-hand merely (as they appear to the animals which are not human). *Ens ut primum cognitum,* "Firstness", does no more than establish the foundation for the eventual arising of questions of the form, "What is that?" Here is the point of transformation whereat generically animal Umwelt becomes species-specifically human Lebenswelt.[33]

Hence is the human animal able to visualize the difference within objectivity and experience between a nonexistent object as such and an existent one, even though in a given case a given individual may be hard pressed to know whether a given object is real, or may be entirely deceived on the point. It is enough sometimes to experience the difference between objects signified as existing which turn out not to exist and objects signified as not existing which turn out to exist (in other words, it is enough to have uncovered or, better still, to have successfully purveyed, a lie) in order to be in a position to ponder the nature of the case.[34]

Other than human animals, of course, also experience errors and deceits.[35] But they have no way of thematizing the origin of such experiences in the objective difference between structures of objectivity which go beyond, in contrast to those which wholly fall within, the direct experience. In this apprehension reflection is involved, but is not the original source of the differential apprehension. On this point the *Tractatus de*

---

[33] Cf. Peirce c.1890: CP 1.357; and Guagliardo 1993 and 1994.

[34] Aristotle, c.348–330BC, Met. VII, 1635, continuing the discussion from Ch. 1, note 16, p. 13 above, italics added: "when we come to the concrete thing . . . when they go out of our actual consciousness it is not clear whether they exist or not; *but they are always stated and cognized by means of the universal formula.*"

[35] In particular, see Sebeok 1981.

Signis text is both quite clear and very insistent.[36] The reason given is the fact that "a cognition whereby a mind-dependent aspect of objectivity is itself denominated cognized reflexively as a point to be thematized supposes the already formed mind-dependent being, since indeed the reflexive awareness is borne upon that being as upon the terminus cognized",[37] and the conclusion is summarized with the typically late Latin compactness that verges on opacity:

[36] First Preamble, Article 3, "By What Powers and through Which Acts Do Mind-Dependent Beings Come About?" 71/20–29: "The cognition forming a mind-dependent being is not a reflexive cognition respecting that being as a thing cognized as the object which [is known], but rather that direct cognition which denominates the very non-mind-independent being (or being that is not relative independently of mind) 'known' on the pattern of a mind-independent being or relation is said to form a mind-dependent being. It is from that direct cognition that a mind-dependent being results." – "Cognitio formans ens rationis non est reflexa respiciens ipsum tamquam rem cognitam ut quod, sed illa cognitio directa, quae ipsum non ens reale vel quod realiter relativum non est, denominat cognitum ad instar entis vel relationis realis, dicitur formare vel ex illa resultare ens rationis."
But see further 71/30–37 and 71/46–72/4.

[37] *Tractatus de Signis*, First Preamble, Article 3, 71/30–38: "The reason for this conclusion is clear: such a cognition, whereby a mind-dependent being itself is denominated cognized reflexively and as the 'object which', supposes the [already] formed mind-dependent being, since indeed the cognition is borne upon that being as upon the terminus cognized. Therefore such a reflexive cognition does not initially form that mind-dependent being, but supposes its having been formed and, as it were, examines that objective construct. . . . And it is the same when anyone understands these intentions by examining their nature; for then the very intentions examined are not formed, but upon them others are founded, inasmuch as they are cognized in general or by way of predication, etc." – "Ratio est manifesta, quia talis cognitio, qua ipsum ens rationis denominatur cognitum reflexe et tamquam quod, supponit ens rationis formatum, siquidem super ipsum fertur tamquam super terminum cognitum. Ergo talis cognitio reflexa non primo format ipsum, sed supponit formatum et quasi speculatur ipsum ens rationis. . . . Et idem est, quando aliquis intelligit istas intentiones speculando naturam earum; tunc enim non formantur ipsae intentiones speculatae, sed super ipsas fundantur aliae, quatenus cognoscuntur in universali vel per modum praedicationis etc." See further 76/19–31.

What formally and essentially creates initially mind-dependent being is not, therefore, the reflexive cognition whereby precisely a mind-dependent being is denominated cognized as being mind-dependent, but the cognition whereby that which is not is denominated cognized on the pattern of that which is.[38]

Whence, interestingly enough, if it were the case that reflective self-awareness were required for the formation of mind-dependent being, there could be no sense-perception apart from understanding, which would, in effect, relegate the animals other than humans to the mechanized status Descartes deemed them to have, since it is characteristic of a machine to function only within the order of physical relationships.

The reflective nature of the *Cogito* is not presupposed to, but has its common origin in, the apprehensive modality which constitutes an Innenwelt as species-specifically human. This modality is able to compare within experience mind-dependent and mind-independent aspects of the objective world as a consequence of being aware of the difference between objects related and the relations as such, intelligible, but invisible to sense, through which those objects are related and manifested by signs.

---

[38] *Tractatus de Signis*, First Preamble, Article Three, 72/11–17: "Non ergo cognitio reflexa, qua praecise ens rationis denominatur cognitum ut quod, sed qua denominatur cognitum ad instar entis id, quod non est, formaliter et per se primo format ens rationis."

Chapter 7

The Dependency of Understanding on Perceptual Semiosis

Human understanding depends from the first on zoösemiosis. It originates there, as from a fertilizing soil. Sense perception has already provided understanding with that whole series of objective relations which, in interweave with the always physical relations of sensation as such (i.e., prescissively considered) and behavioral interactions, constitute the Umwelt as an objective world in contrast with, and partially transcendent of, the physical environment. Absent this zoösemiosic objectification, understanding would have no material with which to begin its proper work of discriminating between "appearance" and "reality" in any of the manifold forms and variety of contexts to which this contrast pertains. Reality is not only a question of what *is*, but as well of what *could* be and of what *should* be and what *will in future be*. Any question of "reality", in the context of anthroposemiosis, needs to be precisely specified, for the general question occurs, as it were, in too open a context – that equally of what "is" historically speaking, and of the understanding developing new realities of its own devising implemented socially in the form of ever new arrangements for human affairs, from the affairs of the mind to those of human society, from the civil constitution of states to the technological rearrangement of physical terrain.

Human understanding takes form, therefore, not originally *in contrast to* (as in the self-reflection of the *cogito*) but originally *in an intersemiosis with* sense perception. Only through and on the basis of this intersemiosis does distinctively human perception arise, along with the possibility to manipulate the inner model of "reality", or Innenwelt, to which any Umwelt is correlative.

The human Innenwelt begins, as does any animal Innenwelt, by giving rise to an objective world, an Umwelt, dually rooted in the interaction between physical environment and biological organism. But the action *proper* to understanding within this Umwelt begins by loosening this tie whereby biological heritage wholly determines the organization of the objective world or Umwelt. The loosening begins when understanding reveals within the objective world a difference between physically and socially constituted aspects of objectivity, and develops by exploiting this opening to introduce into the Umwelt varying measures of critical control of objectifications unavailable to sense-perception alone, specifically through the use of signs critically controlled (or thematized) in their difference from the objects they signify.

At this point the Umwelt itself begins to be transformed from a biological and social reality into one that is cultural as well. The species-specifically human Innenwelt begins to be exapted to form the communicative channels of discourse *embodied* in both speech and gestures (and later, as a matter of essential indifference but relative permanence, in writing as well), but *rooted* in an awareness of a difference between, from any given point of view, "what is" and "what is not". The possibility of historical consciousness and of a cumulative transmission of learning – cumulative, not merely through successive generations of socially contiguous individuals, but a transmission capable of overleaping graves if necessary by the means of texts created through the use of species-specifically human language exapted now into written symbols – are bound up with this decisive exaptation.

The partial coincidence and partial divergence of objective structures with structures of physical being within sensation and perception is thus the zoösemiotic basis and ground from which anthroposemiosis takes rise; and it begins not by transcending but by transforming from within the originally biological Umwelt. In its origins modest, yet this transformation is so radical in its outcome that a new term is called for to label it. I have suggested, without any particular commitment to the suggestion except for its reason, the use of the term *Lebenswelt* for the species-specifically human Umwelt. This term suggests itself to me partly from Husserl's original conception of the "lifeworld" as that out of which science and philosophy alike arise and to which they must constantly recur (even though this conception remains presemiotic in Husserl's own work and formulations). Partly also does it suggest itself out of consideration for the syntactical symmetry Lebenswelt as a term allows with the originally German term Umwelt as it has come to contemporary semiotics from the work of Jakob von Uexküll, through the mediation principally of Thomas Sebeok.

However we settle the terminology, it remains that, through the linguistic framing of the objective world, the human Umwelt becomes a uniquely malleable one, a Lebenswelt, open to reconstitution along alternative lines of objectification in ways no other Umwelt on this planet is open. In the human Umwelt, or, as I should prefer simply to say, in the Lebenswelt, possible worlds, even if actualized, are yet seen for what they are as possible.

The notion of primary modeling system introduced into contemporary semiotics by Soviet thinkers ought properly to be identified, exactly as Sebeok first suggested,[1] with the notion of Umwelt rather than with the notion of language. Under such a consideration, the primary modeling system is the Umwelt, different for each species, in ways determined

---

[1]   Esp. Sebeok 1987.

first of all by a species' biological constitution as this channels what and in what ways physical interactions within the trans-specific physical environment become objectified, and to what degree. Syntactic language, the aspect of modeling unique to the human species, becomes thus a subordinate or "second-ary" modeling system. It is the instrument whereby – specif-ically, through lexical markers – is transcended the functional cycle through which all other biological forms relate to the physical world by the movement to extinguish the physical stimulus in its objective protrusion into the Umwelt (by flee-ing or fighting a hostile factor, or devouring a sought one). In this way language makes possible the consideration of alter-natives divorced from the immediate needs of biological interaction, and opens the way to possible worlds different from the actual one of the Umwelt here and now.[2] Such alter-natives underlie the perception of "neutral objects", in J. von Uexküll's phrase,[3] which are capable of being, as T. von Uexküll notes,[4] sign vehicles for anthroposemiotic enterprises of natural science, but which are ignored in all the other ani-mal Umwelts.

Thus we find in previous philosophical tradition, espe-cially in the text of the *Tractatus de Signis*, a little-realized way of grounding the putative distinction between understanding and perception ("intellect" and "sense") precisely in terms of relation. Whereas perception reveals objects as they are only relative to the biological dispositions, needs, and desires of the organism perceiving, understanding reveals in these same objects the further dimension of existence in their own right, "existence in relation to themselves". Seeing the objects of the Umwelt "in relation to themselves" is a mind-dependent rela-tion, but, ironically enough, by the construction alone of this relation does the understanding open the door within objec-tivity to recognition and investigation of physical nature in its

---

[2] It is in this way, I suggest, that is best met the "need to explain in what way alterity is able to infiltrate the very sphere of the symbolic" (Ponzio 1990: 197).

[3] Jakob von Uexküll 1940: 27ff.

[4] Thure von Uexküll 1981: 163.

own right, as an order partially manifested within but, in its rationale, fundamentally in contrast with the suprasubjectivity of the objective world, and possessed of a being and exercising an existence independent of relations to the knower even when and as *also* related to the knower through, and as parts and aspects of, the objective world.[5]

[5] Because of his importance for the development of semiotics, it is worth noting here that Peirce (c.1890: 1.365) considered the relation of identity, "the relation that everything bears to itself", to be "a sort of degenerate Secondness that does not fulfill the definition of a relation of reason", i.e., *relatio rationis*, mind-dependent relation. In this he uncharacteristically missed a main point of the scholastic doctrine in this area, which turns out, in this case of this particular mind-dependent relation, to have a central importance for the doctrine of signs. Indeed Peirce is right that identity, from within his scheme of semiotic categories, is a sort of degenerate Secondness; but this is only after this relation has *already served* the understanding to reach that point where it becomes possible for thought to form any categorial scheme in the first place, and to emerge from the cloud of Firstness wherein there is yet no difference between objective world and the realm of Secondness.

"All degenerate seconds may be conveniently termed internal, in contrast to external seconds, which are constituted by external fact, and are true actions of one thing upon another", Peirce remarks (*ibid.*). This is correct, for the relation of identity in the realm of secondness is a physical object viewed through the mind-dependent relation to itself. But the relation of identity as originally serving to ground the experience between natural and social signs in the difference of their respective objects signified is the primal manifestation of understanding in its difference from sense, upon which manifestation all else follows, from the categories to morality, science, literature, and the works of civilization generally.

The scholastics, precisely because of the identity status (in Peircean terms) of both founding subject and terminus, regarded self-identity as the paradigm case of a purely objective relation, and this view turns out well to befit the role this relation seems to play in the awakening of the understanding to its proper life and difference from sense. For the requirement for a relation that its foundation be distinct from its terminus is here, in the case of identity, met only through the rational activity of the mind itself reduplicating its object through a relation which, outside of thought, i.e., physically, cannot obtain as a relation but only as a subjective mode of being.

Let us take Peirce's own example (*ibid.*), "Lucullus dines with

The classical modern authors, by contrast, despite themselves, have produced a series of texts which severally have as

Lucullus", where the Lucullus "eating" and the Lucullus "eaten
with" are the same Lucullus – that is, Lucullus ate alone. This odd
case of self-relation, or identity, is the paradigm case of mind-dependent relation because it best and most directly illustrates how the case
of the purely objective relation, as resulting from cognition alone, differs from the case of the mind-independent relation as resulting from
a foundation in physical subjectivity (*Tractatus de Signis*, First
Preamble, Article 3, 70/24–71/10, italics added): "*in the case of mind-
dependent relations*, there comes about a denomination even before the
relation itself is known in act through a comparison, owing solely to
this: that the fundament is posited. For example . . . the letters in a
closed book are a sign, even if the relation of the sign, which is mind-
dependent, is not actually considered. . . . In this, mind-dependent or
mental relations differ from mind-independent or physical relations,
because mind-independent relations do not denominate unless they
exist, as, for example, someone is not said to be a father unless he
actually has a relation to a son [but cf. the extended discussion on this
point in Deely 1990: 36–46]. . . . The reason for this difference is that
in the case of mind-dependent relations, their actual existence consists in actually being cognized objectively, which is something that
does not take its origin from the fundament and terminus, but from
the understanding. Whence many things could be said of a subject by
reason of a fundament without the resultance of a relation [for example, the dinosaur bone, on being discovered, might not be recognized
as a dinosaur bone, but mistaken for a rock, if fossilized, etc.], because
this does not follow upon the fundament itself and the terminus, but
upon cognition. But *in the case of physical relations*, since the relation
naturally results from the fundament and the terminus, nothing
belongs in an order to a terminus by virtue of a fundament, except by
the medium of a relation." – "in relationibus rationis contingit fieri
denominationem, etiam antequam actu cognoscatur per comparationem ipsa relatio, solum per hoc, quod ponatur fundamentum. V. g.
. . . litterae in libro clauso sunt signum, etiamsi actu non consideretur
relatio signi, quae est rationis. . . . In quo differunt relationes rationis
a realibus, quia reales non denominant nisi existant, sicut non dicitur
aliquis pater, nisi actu habeat relationem ad filium. . . . Cuius ratio est,
quia in relationibus rationis esse actuale ipsarum consistit in actu-
aliter cognosci obiective, quod non provenit ex fundamento et termino, sed ex intellectu. Unde multa poterunt ratione fundamenti dici de
subiecto sine resultantia relationis [exempli gratia, os dinosauris,
repertum a casu, non necessarie recognosceretur ut sic; posset errate
consideratum ut lapidus, si sit fossiladum, etc.], quia haec non

the inexorable outcome of their logical consequences the arrival at a "no passage" beyond the mind's own creations. Arrival at this impasse was made inevitable not because these authors began their work by giving primary consideration to discourse rather than being, but simply because they pressed their analysis without establishing, either first or at least in the course of the enterprise, an adequate distinction between the sign as a suprasubjective means of communion and its subjective foundation in representation, between sign and sign-vehicle, signification and representation. But, at the same time, the establishment of such a distinction was hardly open to them, since they had already accepted, along with the reduction of objects to ideas as psychological states of the individual knower, the proposition that relations in their proper being consist not in prospectively intersubjective connections among physical things and objects alike but simply in comparisons made by the mind between objects and aspects of objects precisely as existing only in cognition. Thus was semiotic as a field of investigation and possible body of knowledge precluded from the beginning and throughout the period of classical modernity.

Not until the semiotic of Charles Peirce do we encounter again a serious attempt to pick up the Ariadne's thread offered from within experience by the simple recognition that the action of signs cannot be confined to any one definition of "reality"; for no matter how we define the term, or how convinced we may be of what "should" be its primary referent, the sign will refuse to obey the boundary thus proscribed and continue to import illegal immigrants from some *other* realm, creatures with which we will have all the usual difficulties in determining their proper credentials and identity vis-à-vis our paradigm. This is the thread that turns out now clearly to lead to the center of semiotic consciousness.

Another thread is the historical one, for while it is now

sequitur ipsum fundamentum et terminum, sed cognitionem. In relationibus vero realibus cum relatio naturaliter resultet ex fundamento et termino, nihil convenit ex vi fundamenti in ordine ad terminum nisi media relatione."

generally known that Augustine first proposed sign as a general notion, it is only just becoming known that Poinsot was the first to show the reality of such a possibility as a mode of being indifferent to the divide between nature and culture, a mode of being that is realized not only in the sign but in the sign supremely. In early November of 1986 I was forwarded from the University of California Press a letter from Walker Percy, which concluded with the prophecy that "a few years from now Poinsot will be recognized as one of the major founders, if not the founder, of modern semiotic".[6] Vincent Guagliardo, just months before his untimely death at the age of fifty-one, picked up such threads as these to weave an overview which keeps sight of both the forest and the trees through which the historical path leads us today to the center of semiotic consciousness:[7]

> The "father" of semiotics is frequently held to be the American philosopher Charles S. Peirce, who himself studied the Scholastics. But [in that case account needs to be taken of] the *Treatise on Signs* written by John Poinsot, a contemporary of Descartes: drawing upon the thought of Aquinas on signs, Poinsot had already developed a new discipline within philosophy (a need also seen but not addressed by John Locke), laying the groundwork for an entire field of study which has come into its own only in recent years. . . . [Those concerned with the grounding of our knowledge of the physical world] and postmoderns alike, in their reaction against the moderns from Descartes to our own century, can find a common resource in Poinsot's work on signs. Of special importance is Poinsot's view of the foundational nature of the sign, indifferent in its being to the order of mind-independent or mind-dependent being, and so prior to the distinction between "real" and "unreal", pro-

---

6   Walker Percy, letter to the author dated October 27, 1986, and since published in Samway Ed. 1995: 171–73.

7   Guagliardo 1995: 4.

viding the passage between both. Poinsot's semiotics can thus move our thinking beyond the time-worn, polemical conflicts . . . with moderns, offering in their place a new basis from which . . . postmoderns can view and pursue common concerns of our day.

Semiotics restores to understanding its continuity with and dependence upon sense, as the empiricists beginning with Locke sought to establish as against the rationalists, but it also preserves the relative autonomy of understanding vis-à-vis the sense perception, as the rationalists were convinced. Most importantly, perhaps, it accomplishes both of these objectives while demonstrating the full amplitude of human understanding as a symbolic growth in time asymptotically coextensive with being, exactly as was announced in the medieval formula made incoherent by modernity: "being and truth turn into one another" – *ens et verum convertuntur*. But "being" here must be understood not merely in the restricted sense of the physical being or *ens reale* so perniciously translated as "real being" throughout the modern period (if the Latins in contrast to the moderns were bothered with at all), but in the more ample objective sense of those things within experience which, exactly as semiotics requires, turn out on a sufficiently critical examination to be sometimes real and sometimes unreal, but in either event something about which there are truths as well as falsehoods that can be uttered.[8] Hamlet, after all, was not a carefree, happy-go-lucky sort, despite his status as a negation. But were it not for our experience of fellows who had indeed the positive being of subjec-

---

[8] See Poinsot's observation (from Reiser 1930: 594a43–b6, cited in Deely 1985: 474n116) that St. Thomas "teaches in his *Commentary* on the First Book of the *Sentences* of Peter Lombard, dist. 2, q. 1, art. 5, reply to the second objection, that thing belongs to the transcendentals, and for this reason pertains equally to absolutes and to relatives. For in that *locus* he takes thing transcendentally, according as it is common to an entity and a mode" – "docet in 1. dist. 2, q. 1. art. 5. ad 2., quod res est de transcendentalibus et ideo se habet communiter ad absoluta et relativa. Ibi enim sumit rem transcendentaliter, prout est communis ad entitatem et modum."

tivity beyond their mere objectivity in our recollections and fancy, there could be no Hamlet.

Such is the dependency of anthroposemiosis on zoösemiosis, of human understanding on perceptual semiosis, and, more generally, on the semiosis of sensation through which both perception and understanding maintain their constant, if constantly shifting and sometimes evanescent, set of relations with the physical environment that provides the lining for the otherwise purely objective world in which we live and move and have our being.

Chapter 8

Language and Understanding as a Single Semiosis Exapted

Certainly the thread that we have followed in these pages leads to the center of semiotic consciousness if, indeed, there is a way of interpreting the difference between "sense" and "intellect" anything like what has been outlined here that is decisive for semiotics. For within the interweave and flux in experience of cognition-dependent and cognition-independent relations, only those organisms possessing the capacity to understand in its distinction from the capacities to sense and perceive, in the way just described, will ever be able even on occasion, on this planet or on a planet elsewhere in the physical environs, to discriminate between real and unreal elements in semiosis, the process of communication through signs.

Stipulation, the use of signs as an arbitrary medium such as Saussure made the basis of scientific linguistics and as a distinctive semiotic process, presupposes exactly this ability; and it is *only* in relation to stipulative decisions and their consequences that language, as "conventional", can be said to be species-specifically human. But stipulations presuppose an ability to use signs grasped directly in terms of the relations which constitute them, as occurs only in anthroposemiosis, and stipulations, when successful, pass into customs, and customs into nature. Thus, sign-systems arise out of nature in anthropoid experience, become partially mind-dependent through the transcendence of physical environment and transformation of it into an objective world in perception, and then partially "conventionalized" in the sphere of human understanding, as the social relations of immediate interactions among coeval conspecifics become wrapped up with cultural relations. Through these latter relations alone, from calendars to courts to compacts, wherein history begins to accumulate in a modality transmissible independently of biological inheritance, does it come about that anthropos, the human animal, is no longer tied to immediate interactions. But the conventional in this sense then passes back again through customs into continuity with the natural world as it is experienced perceptually by human and non-human animals alike.[1]

"Language", in short, in the sense that is species-specific to *homo sapiens*, is nothing else than the purely objective component of semiosis explicitly segregated and seized upon in its unique signifying potential by the understanding in its distinction from perception and sense. As a result of the exaptation of language so constituted and brought into play, those organisms capable of seizing upon the difference between the comparatively pure and mixed elements of objectivity soon find themselves in a world different from their animal brethren of even the most kindred biological species. In pre-linguistic experience, relations are not distinguished from the *objects related*. With syntactic language, it becomes possible to separate the two (as, indeed, with the unreflected apprehension of this difference syntactic language becomes possible). The consequences of this simple feat are enormous, and

---

[1] This was the implicit point in the rejection within the *Tractatus de Signis* text, Book II, Questions 5 and 6, of the dichotomous division of signs into "natural" and "conventional" in favor of a trichotomy of "stipulated-customary-natural" in which, as is typical of semiotic trichotomies, each term is capable of passing into the other. See Deely 1978: esp. 7ff.

without end – literally, for it is this, as we earlier noted,[2] that makes human experience an "open-ended" affair (an "infinite semiosis") as a matter of principle and capable of giving rise to that whole panoply of postlinguistic structures that we are accustomed to call "culture". This whole point has been nicely captured in a formulation by Floyd Merrell:[3] "if a dog and the idea of a dog were separate", two subjectivities, let us say, one psychological and one biological, "then there would be a relation between them, and therefore an idea of this relation, and so on, *ad infinitum*" – on condition only that an organism, some organism, be capable of apprehending and playing with the relation as such. Absent that condition, and the *ad infinitum* disappears on the side of objectivity.

My remarks above about the contemporary notion of modeling systems, so richly explored by Anderson in the Special Session she organized for the thirteenth Annual Meeting of the Semiotic Society of America[4] and, later, in the huge work she and Floyd Merrell assembled,[5] have perhaps already been enough to indicate the contemporary relevance of the text of Poinsot's *Tractatus de Signis* (emblematic in this particular of the larger relevance of Latin semiotics in general[6]). Suffice it to say that if we translate the underdeveloped grounding of the understanding/sense-perception distinction to be found among the Latins into what I would call postmodern terms (all properly semiotic terms are postmodern, because they deal with a problematic that inherently transcends the limits of the classical modern epistemological paradigm), we find that the text of the *Tractatus de Signis* has among its contemporary implications something very like what Sebeok remarks in the following passage:[7]

---

2   See, in Chapter 6 above, p. 92, text and note 21.
3   Merrell 1988: 257.
4   Anderson 1988; Salthe and Anderson 1988.
5   Merrell and Anderson 1991.
6   See Beuchot and Deely 1995.
7   Sebeok 1987: 24.

Language is itself properly speaking a secondary modeling system, not a primary modeling system, by virtue of the all but singular fact that it incorporates a syntactic component, while there are as far as we know no other zoösemiotic[8] systems that do so, although this feature does abound in endosemiotic systems.[9] . . . Syntax makes it possible for hominids not only to represent immediate reality[10] . . . but also to uniquely frame an indefinite number of possible worlds. . . . Thus man is able to fabricate a tertiary modeling system of the sort that John Tyler Bonner calls "true culture", . . . what the Moscow-Tartu group has traditionally been calling a secondary modeling system.

And what *Introducing Semiotic* called post-linguistic structures.[11] Language, like the species-specifically human *Umwelt* itself, is rooted in the *Innenwelt*, whence it is transcribed, so to speak, or, better, transcoded, into the structures of the *Umwelt*, where it exists as publically accessible, indeed, but only to conspecifics, which means, in this case, cognitive organisms (whether from this planet or elsewhere) possessed of the capacity of understanding in its difference from sense in the manner these chapters have undertaken to describe.

---

[8]   The umlaut is added, since Sebeok normally spells the word incorrectly (although in accordance with its original coinage).

[9]   This fact, in terms of the *Tractatus de Signis* text (Book I, Question 1, 126/1–18), would be explained through virtual semiosis, itself rooted, no less than actual semiosis among animals, in the unique feature of relation whereby, as a suprasubjective mode of being, it has no direct intrinsic tie to actual subjectivity, but only an indirect one (through foundation or termination), as we have seen. This notion of virtual semiosis is developed principally in Deely 1990: 83–95, under the label "physiosemiosis". See also the remarks of Max Fisch, p. 67 above.

[10] I.e., the cross-section of physically actual surroundings here and now to which the organism is cognitively attuned in its sense perceptions.

[11] The idea was originally broached in Deely 1980.

Chapter 9

The Semiotic Animal

Crucial to understanding the intersemioticity of the early modern *Tractatus de Signis* of late Latin tradition and postmodern contemporary semiotic formulations are the distinction between language and communication, and the notion of human language used for communication as an exaptation rather than an adaptation of any pre-existing zoösemiotic system as such.[1] But central to both these formulations is the point that this book in the reader's hand has been concerned to establish: the point that anthroposemiosis consists specifically in an intersemiosis of perception and understanding whereby the intrinsic indifference of the action of signs to the signification of what is or is not at any given moment is, through an explicit realization, brought to its highest exercise. In this exercise it reaches finally the level at which it can be itself thematized and explored on its own terms, terms which turn out to be the very terms of semiosis itself.

If, therefore, semiotics is that knowledge that arises from observation and reflection upon the action of signs, as biology is that knowledge that arises from observation and reflection upon the activity of organisms; and if semiotics has as its

---

[1]   See especially Sebeok 1985, 1986a and 1991.

principal upshot the realization that, together with the experiences upon which human knowledge depends, all of human knowledge in whatever field develops through this action which semiotics thematizes, then we can see in terms of genus and difference the definition of human nature that semiotics calls for. The human animal, as the only animal that, besides making and making use of signs, knows that there are signs, is properly called *animal semeioticum*, the *semiotic animal*.

This definition will serve to mark for future generations the transition from modern to postmodern thought, even as Descartes' definition of the human as a *res cogitans* served to mark the transition from ancient and medieval thought (inasmuch as the Greeks and Latins alike concurred in defining the human being as the *animal rationale*) to rationalistic and empiricist modern thought.

This new definition has a twofold symbolicity. It symbolizes the recovery of that possibility of an understanding of physical and natural being which the Greeks and the Latins prized but which the moderns had ruled out in consequence of their epistemological paradigm. And it symbolizes at the same time the realization constitutive of semiotic consciousness: that the action of signs as resulting in anthroposemiosis provides the sole means whereby the mind has the possibility of "becoming all things" – *anima est quoddamodo omnia* – in that convertibility of being with truth that is the elusive, asymptotic goal of the community of inquirers needed to support intelligence in those scientific and literary aspects found as expressions only of a race of semiotic animals.

In saying that the human being is the semiotic animal, we give voice to the realization that the human animal is the only animal that knows that there are signs as well as makes use of them. In such knowledge the human being realizes the source of its difference from the other life forms, the *humanitas* of the human animal, as well as the universality of the process on which all the life forms depend. It would now appear that this process is perhaps the ultimate source of that general progress in physical nature from simple to complex forms that we have heretofore called "evolution".

Appendix

Definition of Umwelt

The term "Umwelt", ostensibly German, has been both recurrent and central in the chapters of this book. The reader may feel that he or she is being subjected unnecessarily to jargon, where some straightforward English term could just as well be or have been employed. Such a reaction would be understandable, but seriously misguided.

Need for a Definition

The term Umwelt is less a German word than a technical expression on its own within the confines of the doctrine of signs. In order to show how this is so, an examination of the term etymologically (its origin and history) and in its specifically semiotic sense (its technical definition) is called for here.

If we look simply to everyday German in order to grasp the semiotic sense of the term Umwelt we do not get very far. Since about 1970, the term has been used in the political context of German "green" politics to signify the physical environment, which the Umwelt emphatically is not (even though it includes elements and aspects thereof objectively). Even as a German term, "Umwelt" seems to date back only to 1800, making its first appearance in the poetic context of an ode in German concerning Napoleon. The author of this ode, a bilingual Dane named Jens Baggesen (1764–1826),[1] moved in the literary circles of Schiller, Goethe, Fichte, Mme de Staël; so it is not surprising that his coinage, unspecific as it was, yet found enough resonance in intellectual culture to enter the dictionary. Hippolyte Taine (1828–1893) gave the term a sociological sense in the nineteenth century, and in the early twentieth century the term acquired psychological and pedagogical overtones as well.

The seed for the term Umwelt in its distinctively semiotic sense, however, was not planted till the early twentieth century, in the biological investigations of Jakob von Uexküll (1864–1944).[2] By comparison with usages existing at the time of his work, von Uexküll's originality in deploying the term Umwelt theoretically to illumine his biological research into the life cycle of animals can hardly be overestimated. Von Uexküll's work would prove seminal for semiotics, yet it remains that von Uexküll himself was rather what Sebeok calls a "cryptosemiotician" than a semiotician proper.[3] Sebeok himself introduced the notion Umwelt directly into what now appears as the postmodern development of the doctrine of signs, insofar as that development is called (mainly after Peirce) "semiotics". In Sebeok's writings, Umwelt appears principally not at all as a German word but as a technical

---

[1] Baggesen 1800: 102. The brief summary I here make concerning the origin and history of the term Umwelt I owe entirely to researches communicated to me by the Danish semiotician, Frederik Stjernfelt. "The funny thing is", Stjernfelt remarks (correspondence of 24 February 2001), "that the great Danish dictionary *Ordbog over det danske Sprog* takes Danish 'omverden' to be translated into Danish from German by Baggesen. So it seems that he is the progenitor of the German as well as the Danish version of the word."

[2] See J. von Uexküll 1899–1940, esp. 1920, 1934, and 1940; also T. von Uexküll 1981, 1982.

[3] Sebeok 1976: x, 1977; see the discussion in Deely 1990: 119ff., text and notes.

expression clarifying the requirements for the doctrine of signs pertaining to the life of animal organisms.[4]

What caught Sebeok's notice in von Uexküll's creative appropriation of the term Umwelt was that it unfailingly concerned "biological foundations that lie at the very epicenter of the study of both communication and signification in the human animal", as well as every other species of animal. Only in the wake of Sebeok's appropriation for semiotics of the cryptosemiotic researches of von Uexküll did the term Umwelt begin its life as a *terminus technicus* explicitly in the development of the doctrine of signs. For this reason, in defining Umwelt here, I do so not as much on the basis of von Uexküll's own writings (still less in terms of the historical sources and neo-Kantian resources upon which he drew) as on the basis of those few recent works which develop the concept of Umwelt as Sebeok took it up for semiotics, and – above all – aim to make its sense plain so far as concerns discerning human understanding within the action of signs.

In picking up the term from Sebeok's work, I have found Umwelt to be a key term for the project of developing the epistemological paradigm proper to the way of signs, which overcomes in the process the modern paradigm definitive of the way of ideas. To this end, my effort is so to explain the term Umwelt (so to define it) as to adumbrate and illustrate the line of intellectual development most promising for the foreseeable future of semiotics as fulfilling Locke's prophecy of a "new sort of Logick and Critick". For the way of signs can be traversed only through a definitive breaking out and moving beyond the confinement of modern philosophy that resulted from its pursuit (up to and including Kant) of a way preclusive of that very intersection of nature with culture whence semiotics takes its distinctive "point de départ". My

---

[4] It thus demarcates an area of research midway between the human use of signs ("anthroposemiosis") and identification of sign-functions in the "vegetative" world ("phytosemiosis"), functioning, so to speak, as the keystone in the arc of research called "biosemiotics", itself a step removed from what is arguably the 'final frontier' in our understanding of semiosis, the putative proposal of a so-called "physiosemiosis": see the debate in Nöth 2001.

aim, then, is simply and directly to explicate and influence the *usage itself* of the term Umwelt within semiotics as a contribution to the establishment, little by little, of an epistemological paradigm "home grown" from reflection directly on the being and action proper to signs as the fundamental and universal vehicles by which experience grows and on which knowledge within experience depends.

Perhaps a term posterior to the days of Locke and Hume, even of Kant, is the more helpful in shaping the epistemological paradigm proper to signs in their distinctive action. For neither the terms of modern philosophy, nor also (as Poinsot was the first to warn us[5]) the prior terms of the era of Peirce's beloved "scholastic realism", are adequate to express the point of departure from and perspective within which a doctrine of signs can assume its true visage and form. The scholastic realists were preoccupied with the possibilities of understanding being as exercisable independently of the human mind. The moderns came to be inversely preoccupied with the contribution and shaping of the mind itself in the content of what little we eventually come to "understand" as well as in the great deal we prove to "misunderstand". Yet it is neither in the workings of nature apart from mind nor in the workings of culture through the mind that the sign "in general" performs its distinctive task so much as at that crossroads of nature and culture that we call human experience, whence sound theorizing arises and to which it must constantly recur. Though signs mark paths variously deep into both realms, the sign itself in its proper being is preclusively native to neither realm, is always "mixed" in its ontogeny – at least as it comes to be a reflexive instrument within anthroposemiosis, where alone we first and initially grasp it as such for further specifications.

A term, then, such as our "Umwelt", that admits of no full predecessor (neither in the earlier ages of philosophy nor in the dictionaries of current usage), one that at the same time lends itself to expressing in multiple contexts the proper significate

5   Poinsot, *Tractatus de Signis* 1632: 118/6–9. See the entry "Realism" in the Index to Deely 2001: 977.

outcome of semiosis as giving rise to the web of experience which sustains objects perceived and understood alike, is a term singularly suitable to the needs of semiotics in arriving at the paradigm proper to itself. From this perspective, even the "ultra-modern" epistemological paradigm developed in work of Kant, so much admired by Jakob von Uexküll, is a *passus extra viam*. For even though the Innenwelt to which every Umwelt corresponds is a pre-eminently Kantian structure,[6] yet the Umwelt itself as public, both intraspecifically and (in more limited ways) extraspecifically as well, is irreducibly *other* than the individual privacy of the Innenwelt as a constitutive of subjectivity, and irreducibly *inclusive* objectively of something of the physical environment's subjectivities of individualities as well (which inclusion Kant's paradigm finally precluded, after all). The whole of the public realm, even (within that branch of anthroposemiosis we call "science" particularly) that shifting line between what of the physical environment is objective as well as physical and subjective, is sustained objectively as terminus of the suprasubjective relations through which the action proper to signs achieves its outcomes.

So it gradually dawned on me that inasmuch as the semiotic usage of the term Umwelt is less borrowed than it is indigenous to the nascent doctrine of signs, a *primum desideratum* for the developing discourse would be an explicitly and thematically semiotic definition of Umwelt, an exposition both taken from what there is of established semiotic usage in this area and expressive of the main lines of further research that usage suggests.

The occasion to attempt formulation of such a definition was provided by Kalevi Kull's invitation to contribute an entry on Umwelt for the Special Issue of *Semiotica* in his

---

[6] Kant was the philosopher who best understood the limiting functions of psycho-biological constitution upon knowledge, so it is hardly to be wondered at that von Uexküll saw himself indebted philosophically to Kant above all in his creative research within biology, presciently labeled "Umweltsforschung".

charge as Guest Editor.[7] I had a further opportunity to try out the definition in an oral presentation (with handouts) to an audience of which both Kalevi Kull and Thomas Sebeok himself were members.[8] The following October, as Visiting Professor of Semiotics at Helsinki University, I also gave three days of lectures in Estonia for the semiotics program at Tartu University. Kalevi Kull took me in that period to see the very house on the Baltic shore where von Uexküll wrote his celebrated *Bedeutungslehre,* wherein he introduced for postmodernity to savor this central concept of Umwelt as "the objective world" (as we now see) in contrast alike to the subjective universe of psychological states (the *Innenwelt*) and to the no-less-subjective physical universe of things-in-themselves. From the Baltic shore which lay beneath the window of that house in which von Uexküll wrote I fished a stone from under the shore waters. This stone, thus, carries a twofold story. There is the natural one a geologist might verify: Yes, this is indeed a stone from the Baltic region. And a second story which forever eludes the geologist, the story that this stone comes from within the Umwelt wherein von Uexküll brought to light the structure of experience shared by all the animals, which differentiates them as such from the plants, and which is true of human animals as well. Both stories are true (or false). It is an excellent starting point, perhaps the best so far, to explain the human use of signs in its uniqueness. The two stories associated with my stone as their vehicle well symbolize the dual structure of the Umwelt as an interweaving of relations which reduce on one side to mind-dependent being, and on another side to mind-independent being, but which only together constitute this stone as an item of the Lebenswelt of semiotics

---

7   Kull 2001; Deely 2001a.

8   The occasion was my June 17 presentation "Umwelt" in the "Hommage à Thomas A. Sebeok, 80 Years: 'From Fennougrian Studies to Biosemiotics'," within the framework of the Nordic Baltic Summer Institute for Semiotic and Structural Studies, Imatra, Finland, 14–21 June 2000.

today in which we have a role as participants in its development within nascently postmodern intellectual culture.
My definition, which follows, is a little long by dictionary
standards, but short enough for the purposes of an encyclo-
pedic dictionary at least. I present it here for the reader of the
foregoing chapters as a kind of synthesis of my attempt to re-
establish in semiotic context the sense of the proper distinction to be made (in traditional terms) between "sense" and
"intellect", or, as I prefer to say (semioticians being on the
whole more comfortable with triads), between sensation, perception, and understanding.

The Definition

To begin with, in order to acquire the semiotic sense of our
term Umwelt, we need firmly to note that its *signatum* (its
definiendum) belongs first of all to zoösemiotics, and to anthroposemiotics only from there. In other words, the Umwelt is
first of all, even within semiotics, a vehicle for expressing
especially the role of biological heritage in the use and function of signs, rather than for expressing what is species-specifically human in the use and function of signs. What von
Uexküll as cryptosemiotician uniquely realized, and Sebeok
as semiotician uniquely emphasized, was that the physical
environment, in whatever sense it may be said to be the
"same" for all organisms (we are speaking, of course, of the
environment on earth, though much of what we say could be
applied, *mutatis mutandis*, to biospheres on other planets
should – when – such eventually be found), is not the world
in which any given species as such actually lives out its life.
No. Each biological life-form, by reason of its distinctive bodily constitution (its "biological heritage", as we may say), is
suited only to certain parts and aspects of the vast physical
universe. And when this "suitedness to" takes the bodily form
of cognitive organs, such as are our own senses, or the often
quite different sensory modalities discovered in other life-
forms, then those aspects and only those aspects of the physical environment which are proportioned to those modalities

become "objectified", that is to say, made present not merely physically but cognitively as well.

What needs to be stressed, then, is the limited and partial aspect of the environment of which the organism becomes aware in sensation. When I look out over a rich meadow on a beautiful day, I see what might be loosely described as "an infinite variety of colors". That will do for the poet or even the practical man, but the careful thinker will realize that such expressions are but shorthand for our limitations: we see not all colors possible, but only those that, under given conditions of light and shade, fall within the range of our type of eye. Nor is "our type of eye" the only type of eye. That same meadow will appear variegated quite differently to the eye of a bee, a beetle, or a dragonfly, however much we may suppose an underlying common "physical" being which is "the same" no matter who or what species of individual happens to be beholding the meadow. A rose by any other name may still be a rose. But what a rose is will not be the same to a bee and to a human suitor.

But that is only the starting point in the construction of an Umwelt. For an Umwelt is not merely the aspects of the environment accessed in sensation. Far more is it the manner in which those aspects are networked together as and to constitute "objects of experience". No doubt there are relations among items of the physical environment that have no dependency upon the awareness of beings in that environment. No doubt too that, given the type and condition of my eye, what colors will appear to me when I look in a certain direction will not depend upon my evaluation of anything that is there. If we presciss (in Peirce's usage) sensation as such within our perceptions of the world, it is quite evident that our bodily constitution filters and restricts, but does not by itself determine, what we will become aware of in sensation. If my eyes are normal and a traditionally equipped classroom is lighted, I cannot fail to see the black rectangle against the lighter background that I will interpret as a blackboard affixed to a wall. But what my eyes objectify and what my mind makes of that vision remain as distinct as sensation as such in contrast to perception. Perception it is that transforms sensations into objects experienced, like dark rectangles against lighter surfaces "seen" to be blackboards on walls.

The bee unfortunate enough to fly into the classroom will not see a blackboard. The beetle will likewise fail to apprehend what is so obvious to me, such as the purpose of the blackboard, or the student desks. What objects will the bee or the beetle, or the dragonfly, for that matter, encounter in this same classroom?

That is the question (or type of question) which guided the *Umwelt-Forschung* pioneered by Jakob von Uexküll. Von Uexküll uniquely saw that the difference between objects of experience and elements of sensation is determined primarily not by anything in the physical environment as such but by the *relation* or, rather, network and set of relations, that obtains between whatever may be "in fact" present physically in the surroundings and the cognitive constitution of the biological organism interacting with those surroundings here and now. Nor are those relations primarily of the type that antecede and hold independently of any such interaction. To the contrary. The relations in question are not mainly between the organism and what is sensed (those limited and partial aspects of the physical surroundings which are proportioned to and activative of the limited range of this or that sensory channel in combination with however many other cognitive channels the organism in question is biologically endowed with). No. The relations in question concern above all how the limited and partial sensory aspects of the physical environment are connected among themselves so as to constitute *objects of experience*, and this constitution depends above all on the constitution of the organism doing the sensing. For it is the interests of that organism, not the "independent" nature of the source of the sensory stimuli, that is at issue in the perception as such that the organism finally acts upon and uses to orientate itself within the environment for the purposes of its life and well-being.

In other words, the organism does not simply respond to or act in terms of what it senses as sensed, but rather in terms of what it *makes* of that sensation, what it perceives to be sensed, rightly or wrongly. The female wolf responds to the male's howl differently than does the sheep, regardless of gender. Thus, whereas sensation prescissed and taken as such actively filters but passively receives incoming stimuli, perception by contrast actively structures sensation into things to be sought, things to be avoided, and things that don't matter one way or the other. Yet what constitutes a pattern of stimuli as desirable and to be sought or menacing and to be avoided depends less on the stimuli than upon the biological constitution of the organism receiving the stimuli. Thus, the pattern of stimuli, in perception as contrasted to sensation as such, is actively woven, not passively received. Between and among sensory elements of stimulation, the organism itself weaves a network of subsequent relations which obtain only in the perceiving, not prior to and independent of it. It is the pattern of this network of relations within perception, not any prior pattern within sensation alone, that determines and constitutes the objects of experience so far as they are distributed into the categories of desirable (+), undesirable (-), and neutral (ø). Perception does no more.

In this way, each species constructs and lives within *its own* lifeworld. The whole process is executed by means of signs, but the perceiving organism does not think of the matter in that way. It simply uses signs, as Maritain best put it,[9] without realizing for a moment that there are signs. For whenever one element of experience makes present something besides itself, be that other "real" or not (for example, the danger perceived only through an erroneous amplification of the stimuli of sense), the element in question is functioning as a vehicle of signification. This is why Sebeok so aptly speaks of experience as "a semiotic web", that is to say, a web woven of sign relations, at whose nodes alone stand the objects of experience as experienced, whatever be their further status as "physical" or "real" independently of the experience within which they are given.

---

[9] Maritain 1976.

So it is clear that experience, for any organism, does not simply consist of anything that is "there" prior to and independently of the experience, but only of "what is there" within and dependently upon the experience. So that however many or few relations within the experience may *also* obtain independently of the experience, these relationships have *meaning* only insofar as and as they are incorporated with that larger network of relations constituting perception in contrast to (while inclusive of) sensation, upon whose pattern the appearance of objects as such depends. And this larger network involves relations which would not obtain but for the biological constitution of the perceiving organism acting as interpretant even of what is given in sensation along with, indeed, *within*, the perception of objects as objects.

Now there is a great difference between an object and a thing, however confusedly the two notions are made to play in popular culture. For while the notion of thing is the notion of what is what it is regardless of whether it be known or not, the notion of object is hardly that. An object, to be an object, requires a relation to a knower, in and through which relation the object as apprehended exists as terminus. A sign warning of "bridge out" may be a lie, but the thing in question, even in such a case, is no less objective than in the case where the sign warns of a "true situation".

So we see plainly that while nothing precludes an object from *also* being a thing, nothing necessitates that a given object *also* be a thing. And a thing that is one kind of object for one kind of organism (a wolf, say) may be quite a different kind of object for another kind of organism (such as a sheep), and for a third kind of organism may be not an object at all;[10]

---

[10] In my *Semiotica* version of these Umwelt remarks, circulated in Tartu, "a humble student of geography" at the university there "who is interested in semiotics", Vahir Puik by name, pointed out to me that I had unwittingly, in effect, reversed my own usage of "object" and "thing" in writing: "And an object that is one kind of thing for one kind of organism (a wolf, say) may be quite a different kind of thing for another kind of organism (such as a sheep)." The wording here reflects Mr. Puik's perceptive reading. My original wording mayhap

even without getting into the question of mistakes organisms make about what kind of object a thing is or is not,[11] mistakes which may cost life or limb, or which may in the end "make no practical difference".

To say that an object may or may not be a thing and to say that a thing may or may not be an object sound like simply inverse sayings, but they are not. For to say that a thing may or may not be an object is merely to say that any given element in the order of what exists independently of finite knowledge ("things") may or may not *be known*, whereas the inverse saying that an object may or may not be a thing is to say that *what is not known is not an object*, or, equivalently, to say that *whatever is known is an object*. And since whatever exists as an object does so only within that network of relations (what Sebeok characterized as "a semiotic web" and von Uexküll called an "Umwelt") indifferently from nature and from mind (yet according to a mixture or pattern wherein those relations within and by cognition itself tend to predominate in the presenting of an object *as* this or that), we see at once that "what an Umwelt is" amounts to *a species-specific objective world*, with elements of the physical environment made part of a larger, "meaningful" whole or "lifeworld" wherein the individual members of a given species live and move and have their being *as* members of *that* species rather than some other.

We see then how different and richer is the concept of Umwelt than the subalternate concept of "environmental niche". The concept of environmental niche simply identifies that part of the environment as physical upon which a given biological form mainly depends in deriving the physical aspects of its sustenance. The concept of Umwelt, by contrast, shows us how a given "environmental niche" is merely the physical part of a larger, objective, not purely physical, whole

relied too much on Poinsot's observation that "res est de transcendentalibus".

[11] Or, in the distinctive case of anthroposemiosis, what kind of thing an object is or is not! Again with thanks to Mr. Puik.

which is, as it were, fully comprehensible only from the perspective of the particular lifeform whose world it is, whose "environment" is meaningful in the specific ways that it is ,thanks only to an irreducible combination of relations many of which have no being apart from the lifeworld and all of which contribute to the contrast between the physical environment as neutral or common respecting all organisms, on the one hand, and parts of that same physical environment interpreted and incorporated within a meaningful sphere of existence shared by all the members of a species, on the other hand. Only things which are objects make up part of these species-specific worlds, but within these worlds are many objects which also are not things apart from the worlds.

Von Uexküll compared each Umwelt to an invisible bubble within which each species lives. The bubble is invisible precisely because it consists of relations, since all relations as such, in contrast to things which are related, are invisible. The objective meaning of each world and each part within each world depends less on physical being than it does on how the relations constituting the Umwelt intersect. The difference between objects and things makes mistakes possible, but it is also what makes for the possibility of meaning in life, and different meanings in different lives.

There is yet another way of putting this matter, one which brings more immediately to the fore the dominance of semiotics as the perspective proper to the problematic traditionally called "epistemological". Relations among things always directly presuppose physical existence; but for relations among objects as such, physical existence is presupposed only indirectly. To hit a tree with my car I have to have a car and there has to be a tree. But to discourse about my car hitting a tree I need neither a car nor a real tree. The reason for this anomaly traces back to a little noticed yet fundamental point for epistemology: the status of objects as objects presupposes directly the action of signs, whereas the status of things as things does not (although I would argue that even the status of things presupposes the action of signs indirectly, as a "physiosemiosis"[12]). In Peirce's terms, of course, this is but to say that things belong to the category of secondness, while objects involve always thirdness. But we need not deviate into a technical discussion of these semiotic categories in order to make the point that relations among things always suppose two existents, whereas relations among objects suppose only one existent necessarily, namely, the interpreting organism. For even when the sign vehicle is a physical mark, sound, or movement external to the organism, that which it signifies need not be physical, when the organism is mistaken, for example, or thinking of a state of affairs that is possible ("this hotel robbed") but not yet actual. As when a beaver sets out to build its dam. So we realize that what we have heretofore called objects, and what are yet commonly confused with things, in fact are, as a matter or principle and in every case, significates. To say "object" and to say "object signified" is to say exactly the same thing. The two-word expression merely makes explicit what the one-word expression implies and – all too often – serves to quite effectively conceal from the one using the expression.

To preclude this concealment, and all the philosophical errors attendant upon the failure systematically to distinguish objects from things, we need only to realize that signs are what every object as such immediately presupposes. Without signs there are no objects. For signs are those very irreducible relationships that comprise the semiotic web, and the semiotic web is precisely that network of suprasubjective relationships which constitute objects as such as publically accessible elements of the Umwelt shared by every member of each biological species.

In Poinsot's time (the late 16th and early 17th centuries), the distinction between objects and things and the status of objects as signifieds was explained in terms of the difference between physical relations, which in principle link two subjects (or are "intersubjective", connecting two or more elements

---

12 See Deely 1997, 1998, 2001b; Nöth 2001.

physically existing), and sign relations, which in principle link minimally three elements of which one at least (namely, the object signified), need not exist physically at all, or not in the way that it is represented as existing physically. Later on, in the early 20th century, Peirce would succeed in expressing this situation by a terse formula, or maxim: sign relations are irreducibly triadic, whereas physical relations as such are only dyadic.

We see then how truly Sebeok characterized the species-specific objective worlds which von Uexküll labeled *Umwelten* as concerning "biological foundations that lie at the very epicenter of the study of both communication and signification in the human animal", and, as I said, every other animal, for that matter. I think it is not too much to say that, insofar as there is any one single concept that is central to the study of zoösemiotics, that would be the concept of Umwelt, the invisible bubble or species-specific objective world within which every biological organism that is an animal dwells.

But the concept has one shortcoming, is, we might say, as a biological concept, inadequate in one particular to explaining the human use of signs. For when it comes to the human being, it is true but not enough to say that we live in a bubble wholly determined by our biological constitution. True, our body, no less than the body of a snail, alligator, bee, or armadillo, determines the range and type of physical environmental aspects that we can directly objectify; and our perception, so far as it depends upon sensation, is quite bound by those limits, just as is the perception of a dog, dolphin, or gorilla. But the human modeling system, the Innenwelt underlying and correlate with our Umwelt, is, strangely, not wholly tied to our biology. The first effectively to notice this anomaly in the context of semiotics was again Sebeok.[13] When we are born, or, indeed, when our genotype is fixed at fertilization in the zygote from which we develop, what we can see or sense in any direct modality is established and determined, just as is the case with any animal life form. But what language

---

[13] E.g., Sebeok 1984a, 1986a.

we will speak or what we will say in that language is far from so fixed and determined. Sebeok was the first effectively to point out that failure to grasp the implications of this fact result largely if not entirely from the widespread and long-standing confusion, in learned circles no less than in popular culture, between *language*, which is a matter of an Innenwelt or modeling system that is not wholly tied to biological constitution, and *communication*, which is a universal phenomenon that in and of itself has nothing whatever to do with language.

Thus zoösemiotics studies the communication systems of animals, both those that are species-specific to each animal form and those that overlap two or more forms, including communicative modalities shared between human animals and other animal species. But language is not first of all a communication system. Language is first of all a way of modeling the world according to possibilities envisioned as alternative to what is given in sensation *or* experienced in perception. When such a modeling system is exapted for the purpose of communicating to another something modeled, the attempt succeeds, if at all, only when the other to whom one attempts to communicate such a praeter-biological content is a conspecific (that is, only when the prospective receiver likewise has an Innenwelt which is not wholly tied *omni ex parte* to biological constitution); and the result of the communication (when and to the extent it succeeds) is the establishment precisely of a *linguistic code*, which will correlate with but in no way reduce to elements accessible through one or another sensory modality of the organism. The intersubjective establishment of such a code, then, is the establishment of a new, species-specific channel of communication, to wit, *linguistic communication*, commonly miscalled and thoroughly confused with language itself. That is why, for a communication to be linguistic, it matters not a whit whether it be spoken, written, or gestured: all that matters is the type of Innenwelt underlying the communication which makes immediate, non-reductive interpretation of the linguistic code possible in the first place. That is why the "meaningful world" in which the human animal lives involves postlinguistic structures[14] accessible in what is proper to them only by a linguistic animal, whereas all the other animals, even when they employ symbolic means of communication (as is in fact fairly common), are restricted to the order of prelinguistic, sense-perceptible object domains (including postlinguistic structures only in their sense-perceptible aspects of embodiment).

So the concept of Umwelt applies fully to the human animal insofar as humans are animals, but the invisible bubble within which the individual human being lives as a member of a biological species is permeable to things in a way that the Umwelt of no animal without language is: for the human Umwelt is not restricted to a semiotic web based only on biology. In ancient and medieval philosophy this species-specifically distinctive openness or "permeability" of the human lifeworld was expressed in a maxim: *anima est quodammodo omnia*, "the human mind in a certain way is all things", namely, in the extent of its possible knowledge. In fact, that is the reason for the very possibility of semiotics (as distinct from semiosis) in the first place. For *if*, as we saw, signs consist essentially in triadic relations which, as relations, are always suprasubjective and only sometimes intersubjective as well (insofar as semiotic relations incorporate physical relations within objectivity, as always happens), but are never themselves directly sensible even when all three of the terms they happen to unite in a signification may be sensible, *then* only an animal whose awareness is not wholly tied to biological constitution will be able to realize that there are signs, in contrast to merely using them, as Maritain pointed out as the case with nonlinguistic animals.

So we arrive at a new definition of the human being, no longer the "rational animal", as in ancient Greek and medieval Latin philosophy, nor even the "thinking thing" of modern philosophy, but rather the "semiotic animal", the animal that not only uses signs but knows that there are signs, because as linguistic the human animal is capable of modeling that fundamental reality of all experience which never

---

[14] Deely 1980.

appears to the eyes and ears or any other biological channel of sense: relations as such in contrast to the objects or things that are related; relations as such as the fundamental reality which makes possible the experience of objects in the first place; relations as such which make possible the difference between objects and things; relations as such which, in their peculiar being and irreducibly triadic form, are that which every object presupposes; relations, those irreducible strands of the semiotic web which constitute the Umwelt or objective world in its contrast with and difference from the physical environment as such prior and in some measure common to every life form.

In other words, the human Umwelt is so modified from within by the exaptation of language to communicate that, without ceasing to be an Umwelt, it becomes yet so different from an Umwelt based on an Innenwelt without language that some further term to characterize it becomes imperative. I have proposed that the term *Lebenswelt* should be adopted to express an Umwelt which is species-specifically human, retaining Umwelt to express the generic idea of an objective world which is in every case species-specific consequent upon biological constitution. Whether this suggestion will catch on remains to be seen, and I have rested my case mainly on the three hundred and eleven paragraphs constituting my account titled *The Human Use of Signs*. But while the question of whether my argument on this crucial point will prevail by becoming an accepted usage remains open, the question of whether Sebeok's argument is sound in asserting that the concept of Umwelt is central to semiotics may be considered decisively closed in the affirmative. The success of Sebeok's argument by itself justifies his ranking of Jakob von Uexküll as "one of the greatest cryptosemioticians of this period" in which we have been privileged to see semiotics pass from the status of abstract proposal to successful intellectual movement, perhaps the most international and important intellectual movement since the taking root of science in the modern sense in the 17th century.

Historically Layered References

*N*ote on Reference Style

This work has been prepared in accordance with the Style Sheet of the Semiotic Society of America (*The American Journal of Semiotics* 4.3–4 [1986], 193–215; "Brief Version", *Semiotic Scene* [Winter, 1990], n.s. Volume 2, Number 3, 11–12), as modified to include page-bottom footnotes. This means basically three things. *First* that, barring some oversight, only those works are included in the final list of References which have actually been mentioned or cited, as distinguished from works read, consulted, or relevant to the various topics, as are often included in scholarly bibliographies. *Second* that punctuation marks are placed outside quotation marks except in those cases where the punctuation itself is part of the quoted material, a procedure that follows as a logical consequence of the purpose for which quotation marks are to be used: "to indicate the beginning and the end of a quotation in which the exact phraseology of another or of a text is directly cited" (see Deely, Prewitt, and Haworth 1990). *Third* that all the sources have been historically layered, i.e. (see Deely and Prewitt 1989), cited according to a primary reference date from within the lifetime of the author cited, with the relations to translations or later editions of the source work (the actual access volumes) set forth in the complete reference list. Under the authors of cited sources arranged alphabetically, the dates when those sources first came into existence can thus be seen at a glance, like geological layers in a rock or the age rings in a tree trunk; and since in fact human understanding itself is an historical achievement, the value of this bibliographical principle holds even for purely speculative and theoretical works in any field.

A main merit of this style of reference is that it establishes an invariant reference base of sources across all the linguistic, chronological, and editorial lines of access volumes used – an outcome so useful to the intellectual community as to recommend the adoption of historical layering as the organizing principle for all style sheets.

A specific convention that needs to be mentioned here concerns the dating of the works of authors which can be assigned only an approximate date. In such cases the following prefixes to the assigned dates are used: a. = *ante* or before; c. = *circa* or approximately; i. = *inter* or between; p. = *post* or after. The abbreviation q.v. means "*quod vide*" or "which see", referring to a source in this list of references.

ANDERSON, Myrdene.
  1988. "Knowledge Dynamics: Evolution and Development in Semiotic Environments", in *Semiotics 1988*, ed. Terry Prewitt, John Deely, and Karen Haworth (Lanham, MD: University Press of America, 1989), 3–13.

AQUINAS, Thomas.
  i.1252–1273. *S. Thomae Aquinatis Opera Omnia ut sunt in indice thomistico*, ed. Roberto Busa (Stuttgart-Bad Cannstatt: Frommann-Holzboog, 1980), in septem volumina:
  1. In quattuor libros Sententiarum;
  2. Summa contra Gentiles, Autographi Deleta, Summa Theologiae;
  3. Quaestiones Disputatae, Quaestiones Quodlibetales, Opuscula;
  4. Commentaria in Aristotelem et alios;
  5. Commentaria in Scripturas;
  6. Reportationes, Opuscula dubiae authenticitatis;
  7. Aliorum Medii Aevi Auctorum Scripta 61.
  c.1254–1256. *In quattuor libros sententiarum Petri Lombardi*, Busa ed. vol. 1 *totum*.
  c.1256–1259. *Quaestiones Disputatae de Veritate*, in Busa ed. vol. 3, 1–186.
  c.1266–1273. *Summa theologiae*, in Busa ed. vol. 2, 184–926.

ARISTOTLE.
  c.335/4BC. *Nicomachean Ethics*, in Vol. 2, pp. 1729–1867, of *Aristotle: The Complete Works*, being the Revised Oxford Translation of W. D. Ross's 1928–1952 edition titled *The Complete Works of Aristotle*, the revision having been done under the editorship of Jonathan Barnes (Princeton, NJ: Princeton University Press, 1984); available in electronic form from Intelex Corp. (Charlottesville, Virginia).
  c.348–330BC. *Metaphysics*, pp. 1552–1728 of the same volume (previous entry) in the Princeton edition.

ASHLEY, Benedict M.
  1973. "Change and Process", in Deely and Nogar 1973: 265–94.

BACON, Roger.
  c.1267. *De Signis*, text ed. K. M. Fredborg, Lauge Nielsen, and Jan Pinborg in *Traditio* Volume XXXIV, pp. 81–136.

BALDINI, Ugo, and George V. COYNE.
  1984. *The Louvain Lectures (Lectiones Lovanienses) of Bellarmine and the Autograph Copy of his 1616 Declaration to Galileo*, texts in the original Latin (Italian) with English translation, introduction, commentary, and notes (Rome: Vatican Observatory Publications Special Series "Studi Galileiani" 1.2). (That sounds like a lot, but the elaborate title page is somewhat misleading, inasmuch as it introduces a whole of 48 pp. in all, representing a very small part of what Bellarmine left unpublished in the area.)

BEUCHOT, Mauricio.
  1991. "El realismo cognoscitivo en Santo Tomás de Aquino. Sus condiciones metafísicas", *Diánoia*, 49–60.
  1993. "La percepción sensible en Santo Tomás de Aquino", in *Percepción: Colores*, ed. Laura Benítez and José A. Robles (= La Filosofía y Sus Problemas; México City: Universidad Nacional Autónoma, Instituto de Investigaciones Filosóficas), 11–29.
  1994. "Intentionality in John Poinsot", in Deely ed. 1994: 279–96.

BEUCHOT, Mauricio, and John DEELY.
1995.   "Common Sources for the Semiotic of Charles Peirce and John Poinsot", *Review of Metaphysics* XLVIII.3 (March), 539–66.

BLACKWELL, Richard J.
1991.   *Galileo, Bellarmine, and the Church* (Notre Dame, IN: University of Notre Dame Press).

BONNER, John Tyler.
1980.   *The Evolution of Culture in Animals* (Princeton, NJ: Princeton University Press).

BURKS, Arthur W.
1958.   "Bibliography of the Works of Charles Sanders Peirce", in *The Collected Papers of Charles Sanders Peirce*, Volume VIII ed. Arthur W. Burks (Cambridge, MA: Harvard University Press, 1958), 249–330.

CAHALAN, John C.
1970.   "Analogy and the Disrepute of Metaphysics", *The Thomist*, XXXIV (July), 387–422.
1975.   Personal correspondence dated September 9 discussing translation terminology for the *Tractatus de Signis*.
1994.   "If Wittgenstein Had Read Poinsot: Recasting the Problem of Signs and Mental Events", in Deely ed. 1994: 297–319.

CAJETAN, Thomas de Vio.
1507.   *Commentaria in summam theologicam. Prima pars* (Rome), reprinted in *Sancti Thomae Aquinatis Doctoris Angelici Opera Omnia*, vols. 4 and 5 (Rome: Leonine, 1888–1889).

COLAPIETRO, Vincent.
1994.   "Opposing Mediation and Mediating Opposition: the Interplay of Secondness and Thirdness", in *Semiotics 1994*, ed. C. W. Spinks and John Deely (New York: Peter Lang, 1995), 24–33.

COLAPIETRO, Vincent, and Thomas OLSHEWSKY, Editors.
1996.   *Peirce's Doctrine of Signs* (Berlin: Mouton de Gruyter, 1996).

COLLINS, Arthur.
1999.   *Possible Experience. Understanding Kant's Critique of Pure Reason* (Berkeley, CA: University of California Press).

COOMBS, Jeffrey S.
1994.   "John Poinsot on How To Be, Know, and Love a Nonexistent Possible", in Deely ed. 1994: 333–46.

DALCOURT, Gerard J.
1994.   "Poinsot and the Mental Imagery Debate", *The Modern Schoolman* LXXII.1 (November), 1–12.

DEELY, John.
1965.   "Evolution: Concept and Content; Part I", *Listening* Vol. 0, No. 0 (Autumn), 27–50.
1967.   "Finitude, Negativity, and Transcendence: The Problematic of Metaphysical Knowledge", *Philosophy Today* XI (Fall), 184–206.
1969.   "The Philosophical Dimensions of the Origin of Species", *The Thomist* XXXIII (January and April), Part I, 75–149, Part II, 251–342.
1975.   "Reference to the Non-Existent", *The Thomist* XXXIX.2 (April), 253–308.
1977.   "'Semiotic' as the Doctrine of Signs", *Ars Semeiotica* 1/3, 41–68.
1978.   "Toward the Origin of Semiotic", in *Sight, Sound, and Sense*, ed. Thomas A. Sebeok (Bloomington: Indiana University Press), 1–30. See gloss on the historical caveat called for in reading this essay, in Deely 1982: 214.
1980.   "The Nonverbal Inlay in Linguistic Communication", in *The Signifying Animal*, ed. Irmengard Rauch and Gerald F. Carr (Bloomington, IN: Indiana University Press), 201–217.
1982.   *Introducing Semiotic: Its History and Doctrine* (Bloomington, IN: Indiana University Press).
1982a.   "On the Notion of Phytosemiotics", in *Semiotics 1982*, ed. John Deely and Jonathan Evans (Lanham, MD: University Press of America, 1987), 541–54; reprinted in Deely, Williams, and Kruse 1986: 96–103.
1984.   "Semiotic as Framework and Direction", in Deely, Williams and Kruse 1986: text 264–71, notes 287–88.
1985.   "Editorial AfterWord" & critical apparatus to *Tractatus*

de Signis: The Semiotic of John Poinsot (Berkeley: University of California Press), 391–514.

1986. "John Locke's Place in the History of Semiotic Inquiry", in *Semiotics 1986*, ed. Jonathan Evans and John Deely (Lanham, MD: University Press of America, 1987), 406–18.

1986a. "Semiotic in the Thought of Jacques Maritain", *Recherche Sémiotique/Semiotic Inquiry* 6.2, 1–30.

1986b. "A Context for Narrative Universals, or: Semiology as a *Pars Semeiotica*", in *The American Journal of Semiotics* 4.3/4, 53–68.

1987. "On the Problem of Interpreting the Term 'First' in the Expression 'First Philosophy'", in *Semiotics 1987*, ed. J. Deely (Lanham, MD: University Press of America), 3–14.

1988. "The Semiotic of John Poinsot: Yesterday and Tomorrow", discussion of reviews of and theoretical issues in Poinsot 1632, *Semiotica* 69.1/2 (April), 31–127.

1989. "The Grand Vision", presented on September 8 at the September 5–10 Charles Sanders Peirce Sesquicentennial International Congress at Harvard University, in Colapietro and Olshewsky 1994. This essay was first published in the *Transactions of the Charles S. Peirce Society* XXX.2 (Spring 1994), 371–400, but, inexplicably, after the submission of corrected proofs, the journal repaginated the whole and introduced such extreme errors as to make the text unreadable at some points. The correct version has appeared as Chapter 7 of Deely 1994a: 183–200.

1989a. "A Global Enterprise", Preface to Sebeok 1989, q.v.: vii–xiv.

1990. *Basics of Semiotics* (Bloomington: Indiana University Press).

1992. "Philosophy and Experience", *American Catholic Philosophical Quarterly* LXVI.4 (Winter), 299–319.

1993. "Locke's Proposal for Semiotics and the Scholastic Doctrine of Species", *The Modern Schoolman* LXX.3 (March), 165–88.

1994. *The Human Use of Signs; or Elements of Anthroposemiosis* (Lanham, MD: Rowman & Littlefield).

1994a. *New Beginnings. Early Modern Philosophy and Postmodern Thought* (Toronto, Canada: University of Toronto Press).

1994b. "What Happened to Philosophy between Aquinas and Descartes?" *The Thomist* 58.4, 543–68.

1995. "A Prospect of Postmodernity", *Listening* 30.1, 7–14.

1995a. "Ferdinand de Saussure and Semiotics", in *Ensaios em Homagem a Thomas A. Sebeok*, quadruple Special Issue of *Cruzeiro Semiótico*, ed. Norma Tasca (Porto, Portugal: Fundação Eng. António de Almeida), 5–85.

1995b. "Membra Ficte Disjecta", Introduction to the electronic edition of Peirce i.1866–1913, q.v.

1996. "The Seven Deadly Sins and the Catholic Church", paper presented at the 13–19 July 1995 seminar on "Signs of Evil: The Seven Deadly Sins Sub Specie Semioticae", at the Centro Internazionale di Semiotica e Linguistica in Urbino, Italy; subsequently published *Semiotica* 117–2/4, 67–102, with some revision.

1997. "How is the Universe Perfused with Signs?" *Semiotics 1997*, ed. C. W. Spinks and John Deely (New York: Peter Lang, 1998), 389–94.

1998. "Physiosemiosis and Semiotics", in *Semiotics 1988*, ed. C. W. Spinks and John Deely (New York: Peter Lang, 1999), 191–97.

1999. "The Reach of Textuality", in *Semiotics 1999*, ed. Scott Simpkins, C. W. Spinks and John Deely (New York: Peter Lang, 2000), 127–39.

2001. *Four Ages of Understanding. The First Postmodern Survey of Philosophy from Ancient Times to the Present* (Toronto, Canada: University of Toronto Press).

2000a. "Umwelt", in Kull Guest-Ed., 2001: q.v.

2001b. "Physiosemiosis in the Semiotic Spiral: A Play of Musement", in Nöth 2001, q.v.

DEELY, John, Guest-Editor.
1994. John Poinsot Special Issue of the *New Scholasticism*, renamed the *American Catholic Philosophical Quarterly* while the issue was in preparation, LXVIII.3 (Summer).

DEELY, John, Editor.
1995. Electronic text of the eight volumes of *The Collected Papers of Charles Sanders Peirce*, originally published by Harvard University Press, 1931 and 1958. See on the entry below for Peirce i.1866–1913.

DEELY, John, and Raymond J. NOGAR, Editors.
  1973. *The Problem of Evolution* (New York: Appleton-Century-Crofts).

DEELY, John N., Brooke WILLIAMS, and Felicia E. KRUSE, Editors.
  1986. *Frontiers in Semiotics* (Bloomington: Indiana University Press). Preface titled "Pars Pro Toto", pp. viii–xvii; "Description of Contributions", pp. xviii–xxii.

DESCARTES, René.
  1637. *Discourse on the Method of rightly conducting one's reason and seeking truth in the sciences*, trans. Robert Stoothoff in Cottingham, Stoothoff, and Murdoch 1985: I, 111–51. Originially, this work was not presented as an independent whole but as the Preface to three substantive essays (dioptrics, meteors, geometry) intended to illustrate the method's fecundity.

DIOGENES LAERTIUS (c.175–c.225AD).
  c.220. *Lives of the Eminent Philosophers*, trans. R. D. Hicks (Cambridge, MA: Harvard, 1972), 2 vols.

DIRDA, Michael.
  1995. Review of the novel by Umberto Eco, *The Island of the Day Before*, in the *Washington Post Book World*, October 22.

DOYLE, John P.
  1994. "Poinsot on the Knowability of Beings of Reason", in Deely ed. 1994: 347–373.
  1997. "Between Transcendental and Transcendental: The Missing Link?" *The Review of Metaphysics* 50 (June), 783–815.

DOYLE, John P., Trans.
  1995. *On Beings of Reason (De Entibus Rationis). Metaphysical Disputation LIV*, with Introduction and notes (Milwaukee, WI: Marquette University Press).

DURANT, Will.
  1944. *Caesar and Christ. A History of Roman Civilization and of Christianity from their beginnings to A.D. 325* (New York: Simon and Schuster).

DURANT, Will and Ariel.
1968.   *The Lessons of History* (New York: Simon and Schuster).

ECO, Umberto.
1984.   "On fish and buttons: Semiotics and philosophy of language", *Semiotica* 48–1/2, 97–117.

ECO, Umberto, Roberto LAMBERTINI, Costantino MARMO, and Andrea TABARRONI.
1986.   "Latratus Canis or: The Dog's Barking", in Deely, Williams, and Kruse 1986: 63–73, with an editorial note on the background of this text on xix.

FISCH, Max H.
c.1979.   "Just How General Is Peirce's General Theory of Signs?" in Ketner and Kloesel eds. 1986: 356–61, q.v.

FRENCH, A. P., and P. J. KENNEDY, Editors.
1985.   *Niels Bohr: A Centenary Volume* (Cambridge: Harvard University Press).

FURTON, Edward James.
1995.   *A Medieval Semiotic* (New York: Peter Lang).

GALILEO Galilei.
1615.   Unpublished notes, translated as Appendix IX to Blackwell 1991: 269–76.

GIBBON, Edward.
          Note. Page and note numbers to Gibbon are based on the text of the Bury ed. of 1909–1914, with the equivalences to the chapters and years of the original Gibbon volumes as indicated below.
i.1776–1788. *The Decline and Fall of the Roman Empire*, in the ed. of J. B. Bury (London: Methuen & Co., 1909–1914), 7 vols; chs. 1–14 = I (1909); chs. 15–24 = II (1909); chs. 25–35 = III (1909); chs. 36–44 = IV (1909); chs. 45–51 = V (1911); chs. 52–63 = VI (1912); chs. 64–71 = VII (1914).
1776–1777. First printing of Vol. I (chs. 1–16); revised in third edition of 1777 (=Bury I complete + II to p. 148).
1781.   First printing of Vol. II (chs. 17–26; = Bury II after p. 148 + III to p. 139)

1781a. First printing of Vol. III (chs. 27–38; = Bury III after p. 139 + IV to p. 181).

1788.   First printing of Vol. IV (chs. 39–47; = Bury IV after 181 + V to p. 179).

1788a. First printing of Vol. V (chs. 48–57; = Bury V after p. 179 + VI to p. 268).

1788b. First printing of Vol. VI (chs. 58–71; = Bury VI after p. 268 + VII).

GOULD, Stephen J., and Elisabeth S. VRBA.
1982.   "Exaptation – A Missing Term in the Science of Form", *Paleobiology* 8.1 (Winter), 4–15.

GREIMAS, Algirdas Julien, and Jacques FONTANILLE.
1991.   *Sémiotique des passions* (Paris: Les Editions du Seuil, 1991), trans. Paul Perron and Frank Collins as *The Semiotics of Passions. From States of Affairs to States of Feeling* (Minneapolis, MN: University of Minnesota Press).

GUAGLIARDO, Vincent.
1992.   "Hermeneutics: Deconstruction or Semiotics?" in *Symposium on Hermeneutics*, ed. Eugene F. Bales (private circulation; Conception, MO: Conception Seminary College, 1992), 63–74, followed by a Discussion, 75–78. Dr. Guagliardo was quite irritated that this essay was put into circulation without his knowledge or final revisions; but it is a valuable contribution to the literature of semiotics, an improbable and fascinating comparison of Poinsot and Derrida.

1993.   "Being and Anthroposemiotics", in *Semiotics 1993*, ed. Robert Corrington and John Deely (Lanham, MD: University Press of America, 1994).

1994.   "Being-as-First-Known in Poinsot: A-Priori or Aporia?" in Deely ed. 1994: 375–404.

1995.   "Introduction" to a Special Issue on Thomas Aquinas of *Listening* 30.1 (Winter), 3–6.

HALDANE, John.
1996.   "Intentionality and One-Sided Relations", *Ratio* IX (New Series), 95–114.

HANDYSIDE, John.
1929. "Introduction" to Handyside Trans. 1929: ix–xii.

HANDYSIDE, John, Trans.
1929. *Kant's Inaugural Dissertation and Early Writings on Space*, being translations of Kant 1747, 1768, and 1770, q.v.

HERCULANO DE CARVALHO, José G.
1967. *Teoria da linguagem. Natureza do fenómeno linguístico e a análise das línguas* (Coimbra: Atlântida).
1969. "Segno e significazione in João de São Tomás", in *Estudos Linguísticos*, Vol. 2 (Coimbra: Atlântida Editora). Pp. 129–53 are exposition; 154–68 reproduce selected passages of Latin text. This careful essay, a most important piece of work on Poinsot's semiotic, stands along with the essay of Maritain, 1938, 1943, as a firsthand presentation of Poinsot's views on the subject of signs. It is excerpted from Herculano de Carvalho 1970, q.v.
1970. *Teoria da linguagem. Natureza do fenómeno linguístico e a análise das línguas* (reprint with additions of 1967 work of same title, and now as "Tomo I" with a second volume of the same name published in 1973; Coimbra: Atlântida). "Rarely acknowledged in the English-speaking world" (Romeo 1979: 188–89), several chapters of this work form "a basic introduction to general semiotics" (in particular, Chs. 5–8 "should be required reading as a challenging and fresh outlook on language analysis within semiotics") written "on the basis of and stemming from a wide view of the science of language within the western tradition of studies on the sign", and containing "considerations on both human and non-human communication". This richly learned study was a singularly fruitful result, according to Romeo, of the establishment in 1957 of a chair for linguistics within the Faculty of Letters at the University of Coimbra. "Should Herculano de Carvalho's *Teoria* be translated one day", Romeo muses (p. 189), "crossing either the Channel or the Atlantic, doubtless it will have an impact on a younger generation understandably tired of being led by the nose by those astero-linguists who try to reinvent the wheel each time a Ph.D. dissertation is 'published.' Let us hope his work will not have to wait half a century for a Baskin".

JACOB, François.
1982.   *The Possible and the Actual* (Seattle: University of Washington Press).

JAKOBSON, Roman (1896–1982).
1974.   "Coup d'oeil sur le devéloppement de la sémiotique", in *Panorama sémiotique/A Semiotic Landscape*, Proceedings of the First Congress of the International Association for Semiotic Studies, Milan, June 1974, ed. Seymour Chatman, Umberto Eco, and Jean-Marie Klinkenberg (The Hague: Mouton, 1979), 3–18. Also published separately under the same title by the Research Center for Language and Semiotic Studies as a small monograph (= Studies in Semiotics 3; Bloomington: Indiana University Publications, 1975); and in an English trans. by Patricia Baudoin titled "A Glance at the Development of Semiotics", in *The Framework of Language* (Ann Arbor, MI: Michigan Studies in the Humanities, Horace R. Rackham School of Graduate Studies, 1980), 1–30.

KANT, Immanuel.
1747.   Selected passages from Kant's first published writing, *Thoughts on the True Estimation of Living Forces*, in Handyside Trans. 1929: 3–15.
1768.   *On the First Ground of the Distinction of Regions of Space*, in Handyside Trans. 1929: 19–29.
1770.   *De Mundi Sensibilis atque Intelligibilis Forma et Principiis. Dissertatio pro loco professionis log. et metaph. ordinariae rite sibi vindicanda*, trans. as *Dissertation on the Form and Principles of the Sensible and Intelligible World*, in Handyside Trans. 1929: 33–85.
1781 (1st ed.), 1787 (2nd ed.). *Kritik der reinen Vernunft* (Riga), English trans. Norman Kemp Smith, *Kant's Critique of Pure Reason* (New York: St. Martin's Press, 1963).

KETNER, Kenneth Laine, and Christian J. W. KLOESEL, Editors.
1986.   *Peirce, Semeiotic, and Pragmaticism. Essays by Max H. Fisch* (Bloomington, IN: Indiana University Press).

KRAMPEN, Martin.
1981.   "Phytosemiotics", *Semiotica* 36.3/4, 187–209.

KREMPEL, A.
1952. *La doctrine de la relation chez saint Thomas. Exposé historique et systématique* (Paris: J. Vrin).

KRONIN, John D.
1994. "The Substantial Unity of Material Substances according to John Poinsot", *The Thomist* 58.4 (October), 599–615.

KULL, Kaalevi, Guest-Editor.
2001. Jacob von Uexküll: "A Paradigm for Biology and Semiotics", *Semiotica* 134-1/4.

LAERTIUS, Diogenes: *see* DIOGENES LAËRTIUS.

LEIBNIZ, G. W. F.
1704. *Nouveaux Essais sur l'entendement humain* (first published posthumously in Amsterdam, 1765), English trans. and ed. Peter Remnant and Jonathan Bennett, *New Essays on Human Understanding* (Cambridge University Press, 1981). An alternative English trans. of the Preface to this work wherein Leibniz uses the expression "way of ideas" (p. 301) can be seen in *G. W. Leibniz. Philosophical Essays*, trans. and ed. Roger Ariew and Daniel Garber (Indianapolis, IN: Hackett, 1989), 291–305.

MANETTI, Giovanni.
1993. *Theories of the Sign in Classical Antiquity*, trans. Christine Richardson (Bloomington, IN: Indiana University Press).

MARITAIN, Jacques.
1932. *Distinguer pour Unir Ou, les Degrés d Savoir* (Paris: Desclée de Brouwer). The definitive final edition of this work, in *Jacques et Raïssa Maritain. Oeuvres Complètes*, Vol. IV (Editions Universitaires Fribourg Suisse et Editions Saint-Paul Paris, 1983), pp. 257–1110, was based on the 7th French ed. of 1963.
1938. "Signe et Symbole", *Revue Thomiste* XLIV (April), 299–330.
1941. "The Conflict of Methods at the End of the Middle Ages", *The Thomist* III (October), 527–38.

1943. "Sign and Symbol", English trans. by J. L. Binsse of 1938 entry above q.v., but with footnotes separated from the text proper at the end of the volume, in *Redeeming the Time* (London: Geoffrey Bles), text pp. 191–224, Latin notes pp. 268–76.

1957. "Language and the Theory of Sign, originally published in Ruth Nanda Anshen, Ed., *Language: An Enquiry into Its Meaning and Function* (New York; Harper & Bros.), pp. 86–101, but reprinted with the addition of a fujll technical apparatus explicitly connecting the essay to Maritain's work on semiotic begun in 1937 and to the text of Poinsot 1632 (on which Maritain centrally drew) in Deely, Williams, and Kruse, Eds., *Frontiers in Semiotics* (Bloomington, IN: Indiana University Press, 1986), pp. 5162, the most definitive English version of this seminal text from Maritain.

1959. *Distinguish to Unite, or The Degrees of Knowledge*, (New York: Scribners, 1959), trans. under the supervision of Gerald B. Phelan from the text of the 4th French ed. of *Distinguer pour unir: ou les Degrés du Savoir* (Paris: Desclée).

MAROOSIS, James.
1981. *Further Consequences of Human Embodiment: A Description of Time and Being as Disclosed at the Origin of Peirce's Philosophy of Community* (unpublished doctoral dissertation; University of Toronto, Department of Philosophy).

1993. "Peirce and the Manifestation of Self-Transcendence", in *Semiotics 1993*, ed. Robert Corrington and John Deely (Lanham, MD: University Press of America, 1994).

MERRELL, Floyd.
1988. "An Uncertain Semiotic", in *The Current in Criticism. Essays on the Present and Future of Literary Theory*, ed. Clayton Koelb and Virgil Lokke (West Lafayette, IN: Purdue University Press), 243–64.

MERRELL, Floyd, and Myrdene ANDERSON, Editors.
1991. *On Semiotic Modeling* (Berlin: Mouton de Gruyter).

MURPHY, James Bernard.
1990. "Nature, Custom, and Stipulation in Law and

Jurisprudence", *The Review of Metaphysics* XLIII.4 (June), 753–879.

1991. "Nature, Custom, and Stipulation in the Semiotic of John Poinsot", *Semiotica* 83.1/2, 33–68.

1994. "Language, Communication, and Representation in the Semiotic of John Poinsot", *The Thomist* 59.4 (October), 569–98.

NEWTON, Sir Isaac (1642–1727).

1687. *Principia Mathematica Philosophiae Naturalis*, trans. as *Mathematical Principles of Natural Philosophy* (London). Book I was presented to the Royal Society in 1686, but the publication of the complete work was not till the following year. A rev. 2nd ed. ("editio secunda auctior et emendatior") by Newton with the aid of Roger Cotes appeared in 1713, and the final 3rd ed. ("Editio tertia aucta & emendata") appeared in 1726.

In all three editions, the two words highlighted on the title pages are "Philosophiae" and "Principia", *The Principles of Philosophy*, not at all the qualification of "principia" as "mathematica"; as if to emphasize the mistaken opinion of the period that the viewpoint constitutive of the new science of mathematical physics was the same as that of the older physics or "natural philosophy". We now know rather clearly that in fact the scientific enterprise is distinct from philosophy and not a substitution or replacement for any properly doctrinal development. But just as it took several centuries for the Latins to realize the distinction between philoosphy and theology, so it took the centuries of modernity slowly to realize the distinction between philosophy and science. (See the more detailed recording of these developments in Deely 2001.) Indeed, we even have a name for the historical period animated by the illusion that the new science was simply the old philosophy finally done rightly, the illusion that the new methods of science applied to the solution of all the problems posed by human experience: the period during which it was broadly possible to sustain the illusion in question is the period generally termed the "Enlightenment".

The definitive scholarly text of Newton's Latin work is *Isaac Newton's "Philosophiae Naturalis Principia*

Mathematica": *The Third Edition (1726) with Variant Readings*, assembled and edited by Alexander Koyré, I. Bernard Cohen, and Anne Whitman (Cambridge, MA: Harvard University Press, 1972), in 2 vols. This Latin text, in turn, has become the basis for a new English trans. by I. Bernard Cohen and Anne Whitman, assisted by Julia Budenz, as *The Principia. Mathematical Principles of Natural Philosophy* (Berkeley: University of California Press, 1999).

The history of Newton's *Principia* in English begins with the first complete translation (I omit mention of the several partial English versions over the centuries) by Andrew Motte: Isaac Newton, *The Mathematical Principles of Natural Philosophy*, trans. Andrew Motte (London: Benjamin Motte, 1729), in 2 vols. The main flaw in this first complete English rendering is that Motte did not take full account of the text in the final state Newton left it in the 3rd Latin ed. of 1726. Motte's translation was reprinted "carefully revised and corrected by W. Davis" (London: 1803 and 1819); and became the basis for the "first American edition, carefully revised and corrected . . . by N. W. Chittendon" (New York: 1848, but with an 1846 copyright). A more complete revision and updating of the Motte text was made by Florian Cajori (1859–1930), posthumously edited for publication by R. T. Crawford: *Sir Isaac Newton's Mathematical Principles of Natural Philosophy and His System of the World*, trans. Andrew Motte, rev. Florian Cajori (Berkeley, CA: University of California Press, 1934), discussed in the new Cohen-Whitman ed., pp. 26–37, esp. 29 ff. Thus the importance and authoritative status of the new Cohen-Whitman translation should be apparent, superseded only by their critical edition of the original Latin texts, alongside the first Latin publications themselves of 1687, 1713, and 1726.

NÖTH, Winfried, Organizer
2001. German-Italian Colloquium "The Semiotic Threshold from Nature to Culture", Kassell, Germany, 16–17 February, at the Center for Cultural Studies, University of Kassel; papers published together with the Imatra 2000 Ecosemiotics colloquium in "The Semiotics of

Nature," a Special Issue of *Sign System Studies* 29.1, ed. Kalevi Kull and Winfried Nöth.

PEIRCE, Charles Sanders (1838–1914).
    i.1866–1913. *The Collected Papers of Charles Sanders Peirce*, Vols. I–VI ed. Charles Hartshorne and Paul Weiss (Cambridge, MA: Harvard University Press, 1931–1935), Vols. VII-VIII ed. Arthur W. Burks (same publisher, 1958); all eight vols. in electronic form ed. John Deely (Charlottesville, VA: Intelex Corporation, 1994). The standard form for making reference to this work abbreviates the title to CP, with the abbreviation followed by a volume number, a period, and the paragraph number(s) from which citation is made. Dating within the CP (which covers the period in Peirce's life i.1866–1913) is based principally on the Burks Bibliography at the end of CP 8 (see entry above for Burks 1958).

    1868–1869. Series on intuitive knowledge in the *Journal of Speculative Philosophy*, as follows (from Burks pp. 261–62): 1868. "Questions Concerning Certain Faculties Claimed for Man", 2, 103–14; reprinted in CP 5.213–63; 1868a.

    1868a.   "Some Consequences of Four Incapacities" 2, 140–57; reprinted in CP 5.254–317; 1869. "Grounds of Validity of the Laws of Logic: Further Consequences of Four Incapacities" 2, 193–208; reprinted with revisions of 1893 in CP 5.318–57.

    c.1890.   "A Guess at the Riddle", CP 1.354–68, 1.373–75, 1.379–416 (Burks p. 276).

    c.1906.   Excerpt from "Pragmatism (Editor [3])", published under the title "A Survey of Pragmaticism", in CP 5.464–96. (Burks p. 299).

PERCY, Walker.
    1986.   Personal letter dated October 27; subsequently published in Samway Ed. 1995: 171–73.

PERRON, Paul, and Paolo FABBRI.
    1993.   "Foreword" to English trans. of Greimas and Fontanille 1991, q.v.: 7–16.

POINSOT, John.
1632.   *Tractatus de Signis*, disengaged from the *Artis Logicae Prima Pars* (Alcalá, Spain) and published in a bilingual edition subtitled *The Semiotic of John Poinsot* arranged by John Deely in consultation with Ralph Austin Powell (Berkeley: University of California Press, 1985). The hardcopy is currently out-of-print, though an expanded second printing is being prepared, and the first edition is available in electronic form (Charlottesville, Virginia: Intelex Corporation, 1992).
1635.   *Naturalis Philosophiae Quarta Pars: De Ente Mobili Animato* (Alcalá, Spain); in Reiser 1937: 1–425.

PONZIO, Augusto.
1990.   *Man as a Sign. Essays on the Philosophy of Language*, trans. from the Italian and ed. Susan Petrilli (Berlin: Mouton de Gruyter).

POWELL, Ralph A.
1983.   *Freely Chosen Reality* (Washington, DC: University Press of America).
1986.   "From Semiotic of Scientific Mechanism to Semiotic of Teleology in Nature", in *Semiotics 1986*, ed. John Deely and Jonathan Evans (Lanham, MD: University Press of America), 296–305.

PREZIOSI, Donald.
1979.   *The Semiotics of the Built Environment* (Bloomington, IN: Indiana University Press).

RANSDELL, Joseph.
1986.   "Semiotic Objectivity", a revision by Ransdell of his article of the same title which appeared in *Semiotica* 26.3/4 (1979), 261–88, published in Deely, Williams, and Kruse 1986: 236–54.

RAPOSA, Michael.
1994.   "Poinsot on the Semiotics of Awareness", in Deely ed. 1994: 405–18.

RASMUSSEN, Douglas.
1994.   "The Significance for Cognitive Realism of the Thought of John Poinsot", in Deely ed. 1994: 419–33.

REISER, B. Editor.
1930, 1933, 1937. The *Cursus Philosophicus Thomisticus* of Joannes a Sancto Thoma [John Poinsot], originally published in Spain in five volumes between 1631 and 1635, edited in 3 successive volumes, as indicated by the years (Turin: Marietti).

ROMEO, Luigi.
1979. "Pedro da Fonseca in Renaissance Semiotics: A Segmental History of Footnotes", *Ars Semeiotica* II: 2, 187–204.

SALTHE, Stanley N., and Myrdene ANDERSON.
1988. "Modeling Self-Organization", in *Semiotics 1988*, ed. Terry Prewitt, John Deely, and Karen Haworth (Lanham, MD: University Press of America, 1989), 14–23.

SAMWAY, Patrick, Editor.
1995. *A Thief of Peirce: the letters of Kenneth Laine Ketner and Walker Percy* (Jackson: University Press of Mississippi).

SANTAELLA-BRAGA, Lúcia.
1994. "The Way to Postmodernity", Preface to Deely 1994a: xi–xiii.

SCRUTON, Roger.
1980. "Possible Worlds and Premature Sciences", in *The London Review of Books*, 7 February 1980, reviewing Preziosi 1979 and Eco 1976.

SEBEOK, Thomas A.
1971. "'Semiotic' and Its Congeners", in *Linguistic and Literary Studies in Honor of Archibald Hill, I: General and Theoretical Linguistics*, ed. Mohammed Ali Jazayery, Edgar C. Polomé, and Werner Winter (Lisse, Netherlands: Peter de Ridder Press), 283–95; reprinted in Sebeok 1985: 47–58, and in Deely, Williams and Kruse 1986: 255–63.
1976. *Contributions to the Doctrine of Signs* (reprinted with new front matter but unchanged pagination; Lanham, MD: University Press of America, 1985).
1977. "Neglected Figures in the History of Semiotic Inquiry:

Jakob von Uexküll", reprinted in *The Sign & Its Masters* (reprinted with new front matter but unchanged pagination; Lanham, MD: University Press of America, 1989), pp. 187–207.

1978.   "'Talking' with Animals: Zoosemiotics Explained", *Animals* 111.6 (December), 20–23, 36; reprinted in Deely, Williams and Kruse 1986: 76–82.

1981.   "Can Animals Lie?" *Animals* 114.6 (December), 28–31.

1984.   "Vital Signs", Presidential Address delivered October 12 to the ninth Annual Meeting of the Semiotic Society of America, Bloomington, Indiana, October 11–14; subsequently printed in *The American Journal of Semiotics* (1985) 3.3, 1–27.

1984a.   "The Evolution of Communication and the Origin of Language", lecture of June 3 in the June 1–3 ISISSS '84 Colloqium on "Phylogeny and Ontogeny of Communication Systems". Published under the title "Communication, Language, and Speech: Evolutionary Considerations", in Sebeok, *I Think I Am a Verb: More Contributions to the Doctrine of Signs* (New York: Plenum Press, 1986), Chapter 2, pp. 10–16.

1985.   "On the Phylogenesis of Communication, Language, and Speech", *Recherches Sémiotique/Semiotic Inquiry* 5.4, 361–67.

1986.   "The Doctrine of Signs" with commentaries by Thure von Uexküll and Milton Singer, *Journal of Social and Biological Structures* 9.4, 345–64; reprinted without the commentaries in Deely, Williams, and Kruse 1986: 35–42.

1986a.   "The Problem of the Origin of Language in an Evolutionary Frame", *Language Sciences* 8.2, 169–76.

1986b.   "How Primary a Modeling System Is Language?", in *Semiotics 1987*, ed. John Deely (Lanham, MD: University Press of America, 1988), pp. 15–27.

1987.   "Language: How Primary a Modeling System", in *Semiotics 1987*, ed. John Deely (Lanham, MD: University Press of America, 1988), 15–27.

1988.   "The Notion 'Semiotic Self' Revisited", in *Semiotics 1988*, ed. Terry Prewitt, John Deely, and Karen Haworth (Lanham, MD: University Press of America, 1989), 189–95.

1989.   "Ernst Cassirer, Jacques Maritain, and Susanne

Langer", in *Semiotics 1989*, ed. John Deely, Karen Haworth, and Terry Prewitt (Lanham, MD: University Press of America, 1989), 389–97.

1990. "The Sign Science and the Life Science", pp. 243–52 in *"Symbolicity"*, ed. Jeff Bernard, John Deely, Vilmos Voigt, and Gloria Withalm, and bound together with *Semiotics 1990*, ed. Karen Haworth, John Deely, and Terry Prewitt (Lanham, MD: University Press of America, 1990).

1991. "Toward a Natural History of Language", Chap. 7 in his *A Sign Is Just a Sign* (Bloomington, IN: Indiana University Press), 68–82.

SEBEOK, Thomas A., Editor.
1977. *How Animals Communicate* (Bloomington: Indiana University Press).

SEBEOK, Thomas A., and Robert ROSENTHAL, Editors.
1981. *The Clever Hans Phenomenon: Communication with Horses, Whales, Apes, and People* (New York: The New York Academy of Sciences). An entertaining account of this conference can be found in *The New Yorker*'s "Talk of the Town" for May 26, 1980.

SEBEOK, Thomas A., and Donna Jean UMIKER-SEBEOK, Series Editors.
1979. *Studies in Animal Communication* (Bloomington, IN: Indiana University Press).

STEVENSON, Robert Louis (1850–1894).
1886. *Strange Case of Dr. Jekyll and Mr. Hyde* (London: Longman). The first edition was actually prepared late in December of 1885, but deemed too late for the Christmas book trade and therefore postponed to a January 1886 release. On the original printed copies from Longman, the date is actually hand-corrected from 1885 to read 1886. Note the absence of *The* at the beginning of the original title, commonly inserted in later editions. I have used the text of Michael Hulse, *Strange Case of Dr. Jekyll and Mr. Hyde and other stories* (Cologne: Könemann Verlagsgesellschaft mbH, 1995), 5–78, which is based in turn on the Edmund Gosse London edition of 1906.

STJERNFELT, Frederik.
2001.   Correspondence, with enclosures, on the origin of the term "Umwelt"; dated February 24, March 14, and March 15.

SUÁREZ, Francis (1548–1617).
1597.   *Disputationes Metaphysicae* (Salamanca: Renaut Fratres); in Vols. 25 and 26 of the *Opera Omnia*, editio nova a Carolo Berton (Paris: Vivès, 1861). See Doyle Trans. 1995.

TACHAU, Katherine H.
1988.   *Vision and Certitude in the Age of Ockham. Optics, Epistemology and the Foundation of Semantics 1250–1345* (Leiden, The Netherlands: E. J. Brill, 1988).

von UEXKÜLL, Jakob (1864–1944).
1899–1940. *Kompositionslehre der Natur: Biologie als undogmatische Naturwissenschaft*, selected writings edited and with an introduction by T. von Uexküll (Frankfurt a. M.: Ullstein).
1920.   *Theoretische Biologie* (Berlin: 2nd ed. 1928, reprinted Frankfurt a. M.: Suhrkamp, 1970). Attempted English translation by MacKinnon 1926, q.v.
1934.   *Streifzuge durch die Umwelten von Tieren und Menschen* (Berlin), trans. Claire H. Schiller as "A Stroll through the Worlds of Animals and Men" in *Instinctive Behavior: The Development of a Modern Concept*, ed. Claire H. Schiller (New York: International Universities Press, Inc., 1957), 5–80.
1940.   "Bedeutungslehre", *Bios* 10 (Leipzig), trans. Barry Stone and Herbert Weiner as "The Theory of Meaning" in *Semiotica* 42.1 (1982), 25–82.

von UEXKÜLL, Thure.
1981.   "The Sign Theory of Jakob von Uexküll", in *Classics of Semiotics* (English edition of *Die Welt als Zeichen: Klassiker der modernen Semiotik*, Berlin: Wolf Jobst Siedler Verlag), ed. Martin Krampen, Klaus Oehler, Roland Posner, Thomas A. Sebeok, and Thure von Uexküll (New York: Plenum Press, 1987), 147–79.

UMIKER-SEBEOK, Jean, and Thomas A. SEBEOK.
    Note. The five articles comprising this entry constitute a single, jointly produced, ongoing critique, substantially expanded and – between 1979–1981 – continually updated in each stage or version, that marked a turning point in the discussion of animal "language". The order of the names in this particular case does not uniformly represent priority of authorship for the component entries, as this seems to have shifted, e.g., between the 1980 and 1981a versions.

1979.   "Performing Animals: Secrets of the Trade", *Psychology Today* 13.6, 78–91.

1980.   "Questioning Apes", in Sebeok and Umiker-Sebeok, Eds. 1980: 1–59.

1981.   "Clever Hans and Smart Simians: The Self-Fulfilling Prophecy and Kindred Methodological Pitfalls", *Anthropos* 76.1–2, 89–165.

1981a.   "Smart Simians: The Self-Fulfilling Prophecy and Kindred Methodological Pitfalls", in Thomas A. Sebeok, *The Play of Musement* (Bloomington, IN: Indiana University Press), Chap. 8, pp. 134–209.

1982.   "Rejoinder to the Rumbaughs", *Anthropos* "Reports and Comments" 77, 574–78.

UMIKER-SEBEOK, Jean, and Thomas A. SEBEOK, Editors.
1980.   *Speaking of Apes. A Critical Anthology of Two-Way Communication with Man* (New York: Plenum).

1982.   "Semiotics and the Problem of the Observer", in *Semiotics 1982*, ed. John Deely and Jonathan Evans (Lanham, MD: University Press of America, 1987), 3–12.

VICO, Giambattista (1668–1744).
1725.   *Principi di una scienza nuova d'intorno alla commune natura della nazioni*, trans. as *The New Science* by T. G.Bergin and Max H. Fisch (Ithaca, NY: 1968).

WEINBERG, Julius R.
1965.   "The Concept of Relation. Some observations on its history", in *Abstraction, Relation, and Induction* (Madison, WI: University of Wisconsin Press), 61–119.

WELLS, Norman J.
1994.   "Poinsot on Created Eternal Truths vs. Vasquez, Suárez
and Descartes", in Deely ed. 1994: 435–57.

Index

σημεῖον ix

Φυσις ("nature") 56

acts of the mind 78n9

abduction 8, 35

Abaelard, Peter 20

absolute being or entity 6, 12n18, 24–25, 24n10, 27nn14 & 15, 28n16, 29, 29n18, 31n21, 48n1, 59n15, 66nn24 & 25, 95n23, 99–100n, 118n8

    See subjectivity, transcendental relation

abstraction 23, 166

abstractive 8, 9

Academy 164

accident(s) ix, 28, 55, 84–85, 88, 89, 90, 99

action of signs ix, x, xii, 14, 18, 19, 21, 36, 46, 47, 53, 61, 63, 64, 71, 101n27, 116, 124, 125, 128, 138

    See also semiosis

ad infinitum 122

ad placitum: see *signum ad placitum*

adaptation 124

agere sequitur esse 8

ages of understanding 150

Alcalá, Spain 161

allegory 61

alligator 17, 140

Anderson, Myrdene 122, 122nn4 & 5, 145, 157, 162

angels 71

anima est quodammodo omnia 142

animal rationale 125

animal semeioticum 125

Anshen, Ruth Nanda 157

anthropos 3, 121, 166

anthroposemiosis 46, 78–82, 103, 110, 112, 119, 121, 124, 125, 129, 130, 137, 149

anthroposemiotic 85, 105, 113

anthroposemiotics 132

apes 72, 164, 166

Aquinas, Thomas xii, 57, 69, 71, 117–18, 145, 150, 153

arbitrary, as applicable to sign x, 100n, 120

Aristotelian 5, 20, 57

Aristotle 4, 6, 7, 13, 56, 85, 107, 146

Index

Index